Self-Improvement

NO LIMITS

NO LIMITS

Edited by Costica Bradatan

The most important questions in life haunt us with a sense of boundlessness: there is no one right way to think about them or an exclusive place to look for answers. Philosophers and prophets, poets and scholars, scientists and artists—all are right in their quest for clarity and meaning. We care about these issues not simply in themselves but for ourselves—for us. To make sense of them is to understand who we are better. No Limits brings together creative thinkers who delight in the pleasure of intellectual hunting, wherever the hunt may take them and whatever critical boundaries they have to trample as they go. And in so doing they prove that such searching is not just rewarding but also transformative. There are no limits to knowledge and self-knowledge—just as there are none to self-fashioning.

Aimlessness, Tom Lutz
Intervolution: Smart Bodies Smart Things, Mark C. Taylor
Touch: Recovering Our Most Vital Sense, Richard Kearney
Inwardness: An Outsider's Guide, Jonardon Ganeri

Self-Improvement

Mark Coeckelbergh

TECHNOLOGIES OF THE SOUL IN THE AGE OF ARTIFICIAL INTELLIGENCE

Columbia University Press
New York

Columbia University Press
Publishers Since 1893
New York   Chichester, West Sussex
cup.columbia.edu
Copyright © 2022 Columbia University Press
All rights reserved

Library of Congress Cataloging-in-Publication Data
Names: Coeckelbergh, Mark, author.
Title: Self-improvement : technologies of the soul in the age of
    artificial intelligence / Mark Coeckelbergh.
Description: New York : Columbia University Press, 2022. |
    Series: No limits | Includes bibliographical references and index.
Identifiers: LCCN 2021970037 (print) | LCCN 2021970105 (ebook) |
    ISBN 9780231206549 (hardback) | ISBN 9780231206556
    (trade paperback) | ISBN 9780231556538 (ebook)
Subjects: LCSH: Success—Religious aspects. | Self-actualization
    (Psychology)—Religious aspects. | Technology—Religious aspects. |
    Artificial intelligence.
Classification: LCC BL65.S84 C64 2022 (print) | LCC BL65.S84
    (ebook) | DDC 158.1—dc23/eng/20220127
LC record available at https://lccn.loc.gov/2021970037
LC ebook record available at https://lccn.loc.gov/2021970105

∞

Columbia University Press books are printed
on permanent and durable acid-free paper.
Printed in the United States of America

Cover design: Chang Jae Lee

Contents

Self-Improvement

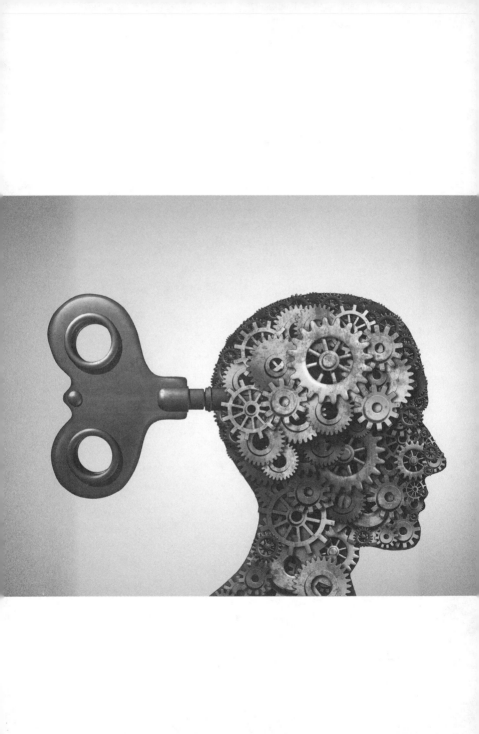

1

The Phenomenon

The Self-Improvement Imperative

We are obsessed with self-improvement. Millennials (Gen Y) and Zoomers (Gen Z), for sure, but also Boomers and Gen Xers work out, meditate, go to therapy, and use apps to improve themselves and their well-being.[1] Improving your looks or going on a diet is nothing new. But today self-improvement is no longer just about beauty or bodily health: we are also expected to upgrade our minds and souls. And the economy reflects that. In the United States, self-improvement is a $11 billion industry.[2] The market offers books, motivational speakers, workshops, retreats, personal coaching, apps, online courses, and so on. Technology helps with this: it helps us to find information, sign up for courses, track ourselves, and let others know about what we do. Like happiness, self-improvement needs to be managed, controlled, measured, recorded, and shared.

But this continuous striving for self-improvement, coupled with self-obsession and perfectionism, is tiring.[3]

Even if people have a good quality of life, they are not happy, because—like in the Netflix series *Living with Yourself*—they want to "create a better version" of themselves.[4] People are restless, anxious, and desperate. We set our goals very high and demand that we soon achieve them. Striving for perfection is stressful: we can never meet the high expectations we set for ourselves, and the speed of modern life is accelerating.[5] We want everything fast, easy, and now. Failure to achieve this leads to self-hate. People suffer from depression and suicide; it is outright dangerous.[6] Self-improvement becomes a personal and a cultural disease.[7] As an article in the *New Yorker* put it, we are "improving ourselves to death."[8]

It is well known that the pressure to perform can lead to depression and suicide. For example, poor academic performance or fear of poor academic performance, which are seen as key forms of self-improvement and means for upward social mobility, has led to depression and suicide among Chinese adolescents.[9] Those in the United States who cannot achieve the American Dream might await a similar fate. Already in the 1949 play *Death of Salesman*, Arthur Miller tells the story of a salesman who chases the American Dream but fails and kills himself.[10] He does so by using his car: a symbol of individualism and freedom. Today this has not changed. Some blame the contemporary U.S. mass shootings on a combination of the American Dream with gun ownership. People are socialized to assume that they will achieve, and when that does not happen, they struggle.[11] Here, too, an ideology of individual success and freedom combined with a powerful technology lead to death. Social problems are framed as individual problems;

collective action and the role of the state and the socioeconomic system remain out of sight. But the problem is not just about achievement in the sphere of study and work, not just about social status. Aided by positive psychology, working on your (private) selves is also a "mantra of American individualism."[12] This self-improvement culture is boosted by social media and celebrity culture. Gaston Franssen speaks of a "celebritization of self-care" which reproduces an individualized neoliberal ideology.[13] Celebrities show teenagers that they have to continuously work on themselves. You have to try to increase your happiness and achieve self-fulfillment. You have to overcome a crisis and reinvent yourself. And think positive! If you feel bad, it's your own fault. You should work on yourself. And work hard. It's all in your own hands. This puts an enormous burden on people, a burden that can crush them.

However, it's not easy to opt out. Self-improvement is no longer optional; it has become an imperative. You have to improve yourself—otherwise you're seen as lazy. It's your duty. And we are always on duty. There is not much room for rest and enjoyment. Just as it is hard to withdraw from the 24/7 economy, it is almost impossible to leave the self-improvement culture.[14] We have to learn and improve. We have to go on. We are self-improving ourselves until we have to give up. We are burned out by our jobs and family lives, but also, ironically, by the self-improvement work that was meant to do something about that.

This toxic culture of self-improvement and perfectionism is not just an American or Chinese problem but has deep roots in Western culture. As I will show in the next chapters, it can partly be explained by ancient Greek and Christian ideas (from Hellenistic techniques of the self to Christian guilt, confession, and the Protestant ethic), humanism's culture of self-examination and learning, and the relentless modern search for authenticity and perfection. It also needs to be put in the context of neoliberal competition, individualism, obsession with self-esteem, a ruthless form of capitalism that predicts and controls our behavior and never leaves us alone, and individualist political ideologies: if collective solutions are rejected, only individual self-improvement is left.[15]

Yet far less examined is the crucial role that *technology* plays, and has played, in the history and culture of self-improvement: not just as a tool, and instrument, to reach our goals, but also in shaping those goals themselves. Modern humanism already had its self-improvement tools such as novels and diaries. If today we have a problematic culture of self-improvement, this is so because we are now propelled by new, powerful self-knowledge and self-improving technologies: technologies that not only offer us information or invite us to reflection, but also constantly measure us and invite us to compare ourselves to others, drawing us into harsh and unbearable self-disciplining, self-surveillance, and quantitative knowledge regimes. An app on a mobile phone to track ourselves, measure ourselves. A social media post and the game to compare ourselves to others. Recommendations and advertisements from companies that have our data and analyzed our statistical information. We are self-improving ourselves until we crash. Some people benefit from it, and technologies are assisting that system. Our self-improvement machines produce self-loathing and frustration. They make it difficult to accept that "you are not broken," as Tina Edwards puts it, and "good as you are"—something we would like to hear from a friend or partner.[16] And this is shamelessly exploited by the self-help business and by the tech and data industry. Our self-improvement time is money: not for us, but for others. As millennials spend their limited budget on self-improvement, self-help authors and tech investors see their income soar.

Is there a way to escape this self-improvement machine? An obvious remedy is to try to spend less time in front of our screens and with our mobile devices. Disconnect. Go offline. But, paradoxically, digital detoxing is itself a self-improvement treatment and a self-help mantra. A digital diet is one of the many self-improvement recipes on the market. And it's so hard to do because it's already so much part of our lives and our world. Given the current ways we work and live, it seems impossible to escape digital technologies altogether: we are already too much dependent on technology. Could there be another solution, one that is critical of our current technologies but not Luddite?

This book reconstructs how we got where we are, analyzes the role of technology, evaluates that role, and reflects on potential solutions. The next chapters delve into how our technoculture of self-improvement came about, why and how it persists, and what we can do about it. It talks about the ideas and the ideologies, about narcissism, individualism, and capitalism, but it also sheds light on the role of technologies such as AI and explores some original, less well-trodden paths out of the self-improvement trap.

OVERVIEW OF CHAPTERS

Chapter 2 searches for the intellectual sources of our ideas about self-knowledge, self-care, and self-improvement in the history of ideas: the Socratic imperative to know yourself, the Stoic techniques to turn inward and make yourself less dependent on others, Christian practices of self-control and ideas about perfection, humanist communication culture with its new, revolutionary technologies and media, and ultimately Rousseau, who stands at the beginning of a modern culture obsessed with the search for, and display of, your true and authentic self.

Chapter 3 examines the modern society that resulted from these developments. It looks at the phenomenon of narcissism and its contemporary forms, the 1960s–'70s counterculture and its enduring influence on our techno-culture, and new forms of existentialism that still shape for example hipster culture today: the idea that we have to make ourselves and that we need to be "authentic." These ideas have not led to a fundamental change of society but to self-obsession, and they have been ruthlessly commodified and commercialized. In this way, the book further shifts the discussion about what at first sight appears to be a psychological phenomenon to a societal and cultural problem.

Of course, people may have their own individual self-improvement goals or not go for perfection at all: they may just wish to be more physically active or look for peace in their daily lives. And not everyone turns away from politics. For example, in the United States, minority groups may see self-improvement practices as a way to resist forms of oppression. Consider Black women's yoga in contexts of structural violence, Asian women taking up self-defense in response to hate crimes, or Native Americans relearning their languages.[17] Yet while I will show how various demographics are implicated in the self-improvement culture (especially different generations), this book is not about the psychology and goals of particular individuals and groups; it is about some problematic aspects of the overall self-improvement *society* and *culture* that result from all that well-meant work on the self.

This move toward societal criticism is intensified in chapter 4, this time inspired by Nietzschean and Marxian thinking. First it questions the political dimension of our current neo-Stoicism: the turn inward seems to divert attention from the unjust social order and amounts to a philosophy for slaves. Then it points to how the wellness industry and capitalist forms of exploitation use and encourage self-improvement to sell us products and services, but also to sell our data. The chapter ends with a reflection on how self-improvement is used for bourgeois class signaling and what, more generally, self-improvement means for different socioeconomic classes.

While the role of technology is treated throughout the book, chapter 5 emphasizes this theme and focuses especially on the relation between self-improvement and artificial intelligence (AI). It argues that AI gives us a very specific kind of way of knowing ourselves and relating to ourselves, which is different from that offered by humanist technologies, and that it confronts us with the claim that it knows us better than ourselves. It also investigates what happens to our conception of self-improvement when we understand it as self-enhancement: what does self-improvement mean when technologies promise to upgrade the mind and the soul?

The next chapters take us on a journey that explores different solutions to the self-improvement crisis: how can we find a way out of these problematic self-improvement cultures, without abandoning the idea of self-improvement altogether and without rejecting technologies? Chapter 6 develops and defends a relational conception of the self and recommends an attitude of turning outward rather than inward: to others, to the environment. But in order to avoid yet another self-help advice, it supplements these recommendations with a call to change society: only social change can solve the current self-improvement crisis. Chapter 7 then asks the question what this means for technology, and in particular AI. Is AI only part of the problem, or can it also be part of the solution? This leads us to a reflection on the relation between technology and culture, and to a perhaps surprising conclusion about technologies, stories, and the good life.

2

The History

Ancient Philosophers, Priests, and Humanists
in Search of Self-Knowledge and Perfection

The ancient Greek maxim "know thyself" was once inscribed in the forecourt of the temple of Apollo at Delphi and was repeated by the personage of Socrates in Plato's dialogues. In *Phaedrus*, Socrates refers to the inscription when he says that it is ridiculous for him to look into other subjects if he doesn't even know himself (229e–230a). For Socrates, knowing yourself meant knowing that you don't know yet, that you still have to learn a lot: it is about recognizing the limits of your knowledge. In the *Apology*, in which Socrates is on trial and in vain defends himself against the accusation that he corrupts the youth and does not believe in the gods of the city, it is said that Socrates is wiser than other persons because he does not think he knows what he does not know (21d). Recognizing your ignorance is the start of improving yourself. Knowing yourself also meant knowing your true nature by recollecting what your immortal soul already knows (that's in another dialogue, the *Phaedo*, also set at the end of Socrates's life) and trying to understand the essence of justice and love. The challenge, according to Socrates, is to live the good life. You need to take care of your soul and engage in self-examination in order to achieve the good life. And as the Stoics stressed after him: getting to know your true self, rather than attaching oneself to external things such as money, fame, and a nice house, is the wise thing to do.

Plato's interpretation of knowing yourself is very different from modern philosophy, where knowing yourself means to focus on yourself as a unique individual. That modern conception is not about knowledge of essences or about the past or about the good life that is supposed to be the same for all human beings; instead, in modernity individuals are asked to construct their own reality and themselves. We can define who we are and want to become. It is not about recognizing limits and your past but about overcoming these, about making your own life and your own future. We will see that this is very clearly expressed by Nietzsche and Sartre: we have to become the author of our own lives. Nietzsche, who criticized Socrates for denying life, thought we should create ourselves and even create our own values. Sartre thought that we are defined by our individual choices: we are what we make of ourselves. Today this belief in radical and individual self-realization and self-creation is coupled with self-perfection and self-enhancement: we want to become a perfect self and enhance ourselves for this purpose.

The idea of self-perfection also stems from ancient times and is part of the Christian tradition. For Aristotle, perfecting yourself means to attain your purpose as a human being. For the Stoics, it is to be in harmony with nature and reason. In Christian philosophy, for example in Augustine, self-knowledge but also striving for perfection is important: perfection is to be without sin and to be righteous, which can only be attained after life and is exemplified by Christ, but we have to make sure we're on course toward it. In the centuries after Augustine, perfection meant to withdraw from the world. Those who chose the monastic life lived alone and later also in community: the monasteries. Their inhabitants practiced asceticism, which means "training" or "exercises." Whereas the ancient Greeks mainly used the term for athletic bodily practices, in the monasteries it meant a simple life, self-discipline, abstinence from physical pleasures, self-denial, and sometimes mortification of the body. This was then meant to create conditions under which one could reach spiritual transformation and perfection: mastery over the passions, rooting out inner sin, and being wholly in love with God. In medieval times, Thomas Aquinas wrote in his famous *Summa Theologiae* about different levels of perfection. Later the idea of perfection remained an important idea in Christian thought. For example, in *The Way of Perfection*, written in the time of the Counter-Reformation, Teresa of Ávila taught her Carmelite nuns how to attain spiritual perfection through prayer in various stages. And while Lutherans and Calvinists reject the possibility of Christian perfection in this life, other Protestant movements such as Quakerism and Wesleyan Methodism teach Christian perfectionism.

One of the sources for these Christian ideas and practices was ancient Greek and Roman Stoicism, which has been highly influential in the history of ideas about self-improvement in general. Its lessons are often recommended as still relevant for us today. For the Stoics, it was vital to try to improve yourself. That meant control your desires and do not make yourself dependent on external things. We should not desire what is out of our control, but we can shape ourselves. By training our mind, we can better steer our desires. You are not external things. In his lectures given around 108 CE, which are transcribed by his student Arrian in the *Discourses*, the Greco-Roman philosopher Epictetus gives the example of a man who has been condemned to death.[1] He has no control over the fact that he must die. But he can decide if he will go lamenting or smiling. He can maintain his character. With a strong will, we can bear hardships. What matters is our attitude and the view we take of things, not the things themselves—these we cannot control. We should work on our character, our virtue. We should not care or be anxious about the opinion of others or about external things; we should do what is in our power. And we have to work with what is given. Epictetus compares this with a weaver who works with the material given and makes the best of it, exercising his art. What matters is that you learn and develop your skills. We have to train self-discipline. Like Buddhists, Stoics recommend that we avoid being slaves of our desires.

Later emperor Marcus Aurelius spread Stoic ideas in the Roman world. In his *Meditations*, he describes how one can try to live a Stoic life in practice. Seneca is also a famous Stoic Roman philosopher. In this *Moral Letters to Lucilius*, written at the end of his life, he focuses on the inner life and the favorite topic of Stoic philosophers: death. Life is going fast, and often we live as if we are destined to live forever, but we will die, and we better contemplate death. Death is always present and closer than we think. Don't waste time, focus on what is important, and be true to yourself: don't live the life that others expect of you.

Next to Stoicism, there were also other schools of thought in the Hellenistic period (after Plato and Aristotle), later followed by Roman philosophy and early Christian philosophy. For example, cynics promoted asceticism and opposition to social norms, and epicureans taught that one should seek modest pleasures, freedom from fear, and absence from bodily pain. Their recipes differ from those of the Stoics. But all Hellenistic philosophy focuses on self-control and independence from the external world. When Greek life became insecure after the decay of the Greek city-states, people needed something to hold on to. The self was their last resort. It was the beginning of an inward journey that would be faithfully continued by Christians and later by modern self-improvers and self-care enthusiasts.

In his later work on the history of sexuality, the French philosopher Michel Foucault shows how in ancient and early Christian times knowing yourself, but also being concerned with oneself and taking care of oneself, were important goals. This was about self-reflection and self-examination, say the Socratic heritage, but also the further development of ascetic practices that were meant to control desire—especially male sexual desire. "Know thyself" here means to engage in what Foucault called a "hermeneutics of the self" and a hermeneutics of desire. Martha Nussbaum picks up a medical analogy in the Hellenistic writings: the Stoics, for example, proposed a therapy for the soul, in particular a therapy of desire.[2] Thus, self-improvement requires examination. This was also still present in Christian practices. But it is not only about introspection, contemplation, or the soul; it also requires exercise and training of both soul and body. It is hard work. In Foucault's words, it is "ethical work that one performs on oneself."[3] Moving beyond what he sees as the "Oriental" emphasis on contemplation, Foucault highlights the performative and bodily aspect of these neo-Stoic practices. This connects again to the original ancient Greek meaning of ascetism: it's about training.

Later in Christianity the practice of confession is added: here the person not only self-examines and verbalizes but also confesses to someone else, the priest. In Hellenistic and Roman times, however, the emphasis was on examining oneself. Since Socrates in the *Apology* urged his fellow citizens to take care of their souls, self-knowledge was seen as the condition for reaching the good life. Moreover, Foucault argued that for the ancients relating to oneself was an art; it was not just about following external prohibitions (and not even, as in Kant, giving the law to oneself) but about shaping a beautiful and good life.

At the end of his life, Foucault came into contact with the Californian cult of self-help and self-transformation, which exposed him to all kinds of erotic and transgressive experiences, including taking LSD.[4] It is in that time that Foucault uses the term "technologies of the self": techniques that "permit individuals to effect by their own means or with the help of others a certain number of operations on their own bodies and souls, thoughts, conduct, and way of being, so as to transform themselves in order to attain a certain state of happiness, purity, wisdom, perfection, or immortality."[5] The normalized and disciplined self that is produced by modern institutions is transcended here and replaced by an active self that is engaged in self-improvement and self-transformation. Like (other?) hippies, Foucault attempted to re-create himself and take care of himself. But instead of looking for Eastern wisdom, as so many did at the time, he critically commented on sources from the Western tradition.

Others took inspiration from Eastern philosophies and practices, for example Buddhism. Although obsessive self-improvement directed at specific outcomes may well be at odds with the teachings of Buddhism and our modern ambitions for self-improvement can be seen as one of ego's demands that should be resisted, Buddhist teachings are often used for self-improvement and can then also be considered as a kind of technology of the self, a practice of self-care.[6] Similar to Stoicism, a key teaching is that one should let go attachment to everything external, but here one also has to get rid of one's attachment to the self as ego and the illusion of a fixed self. This is meant to reduce suffering and eventually end it, since it is believed that craving and attachment are the cause of suffering. We are never satisfied. This is painful. We must liberate ourselves from the endless cycle of rebirth, suffering, and death and try to reach the state of nirvana. Buddhism offers a path and techniques to do this, including different types of meditation, next to exercising moral virtue and gaining insight about the true nature of reality. Inspired by the Buddhist tradition, Western mindfulness practice tries to focus one's attention on the present moment by becoming aware of one's breathing, one's body, and other sensations that happen in the present. Mindfulness was first considered to be something for monks and hippies; today it is one of the many self-improvement ideas and techniques that are present everywhere, from kindergarten to the boardroom.

Indeed, today these ancient notions and practices of self-care and self-improvement are no longer part of a counterculture; they are totally mainstream. More: self-improvement becomes an imperative: *You Must Change Your Life*, as the title of one of Peter Sloterdijk's books says. Like Foucault, Sloterdijk draws attention to what he calls the "sport-ethical" language of the imperative: "You must change your life! . . . Distrust the philistine in yourself who thinks you are just fine as you are! . . . Do not resist the call to get in shape!"[7] As I did earlier in this chapter, he points out that the word *askesis* means "exercise" or "training" in ancient Greek. Just as in ancient times, the idea is to develop a habit through repetitive practice: performative exercise. Ascetic regimes and similar "anthropotechnics" are found from ancient times through Christianity to today. Sloterdijk summarizes the history of these practices. In Seneca's letters, we find ideas about how to care for the soul and the body. The idea is to actively cultivate and perfect oneself by means of various techniques. The Church Fathers borrowed much of these ancient ideas, although they added the goal of spiritual salvation and the idea of pastoral care.

In his posthumously published book *Confessions of the Flesh*, Foucault interprets the metaphor of the shepherd, which is related to establishing a form of communal care:

the shepherd has the power to gather, to guide, to nourish, to watch over, and to give account.[8] The Christian Church, and later the modern state, started governing the souls and bodies of their subjects and exercise the related forms of power in what Foucault called "biopolitics." Here self-care is supplemented with care by the Church, the state, and one could add: the private corporation. Register, and we take care of you. And after Foucault we know that it also means "we discipline you, and we exercise power over you." That does not mean that self-care disappeared. Today, self-care and biopolitics coexist.

Yet under the influence of Protestantism, in modern times these practices of self-care and self-improvement are no longer connected to withdrawal from the world or directed to life in another world. Instead, the focus is on this life and on the here and now. One has to show how well one is doing, that is, how well one is exercising. Industriousness and productivity are important. The Enlightenment added the stress on individual autonomy. The shepherd model is rejected, and there is no longer a renunciation of the self, as in the earlier Christian tradition, or a detachment from the ego, as in Buddhism. Instead, the idea is that people create a positive and unique self. Max Weber wrote that the Protestant, in particular Calvinist ethic, helped to create modern capitalism.[9] But it also supported another kind of entrepreneurship: the entrepreneurship of the self.[10] We have to reinvent ourselves. The self becomes the object of *innovation*. Yes, we can.[11] And this time, we can without the old institutions, without gods, without priests, and perhaps even without teachers. The internet and its social media are sufficient. We can do it ourselves.

Who needs a personal spiritual advisor when we have YouTube?

But, paradoxically, this autonomy is an illusion, since today the state and corporations still exercise the disciplining powers Foucault talked about—now by using digital technologies, including AI. These organizations and their technologies are the new shepherds: they gather, guide, nourish, watch over, and give account, not because they care about us or our self-improvement projects but because they care about making profits with our data. In other words, just as the 1970s hippie practices of self-improvement were quickly appropriated by neoliberalism and wellness capitalism in the 1980s and 1990s, digital technologies such as the internet and AI have not fulfilled their promise of liberation. Instead, at the beginning of the twenty-first century, technologies of the self are inextricably linked to machineries of enslavement. We are allowed to roam the lush fields of self-improvement and try the green grass of the newest self-help techniques, but only as long as we give our data and our money: the herd is under the strict surveillance of the data cowboys. At best, this is a perversion of what Foucault was after, and quite the opposite of the personal autonomy the ancient self-improvement techniques tried to achieve. I will say more about capitalism and AI in chapters 4 and 5.

However, before AI, there was a self-improvement technology most of us are far more familiar with than AI, one that you have in your hands right now. That is the work of humanism, from the Renaissance until now. Like the philosophers and priests before them, humanists tried to create a community of learning and self-improvement, but in contrast to the ancient sages and the Church Fathers, they had new, powerful technologies and media at their disposal: the printing press and the book.

HUMANISM 2.0, OR DIGITAL HUMANISM: FROM ERASMUS TO FACEBOOK

Books are not only a way to tame and domesticate people, as Sloterdijk has argued in his "Rules for the Human Zoo."[12] They are also a technology and a medium for continuing the Hellenistic and Roman tradition of self-examination and self-improvement. Books are used to build and maintain a community of people attempting to know themselves, take care of themselves, confess to themselves and others through reading and writing, and educate in order to improve bodies and souls. They create a collective of those who are bettering themselves and cultivate the *humanities*: the literate, those who perfect themselves, those who cultivate their *humanitas*. They write letters to friends: close friends and imagined ones, members of the cosmopolis. The Renaissance humanists of the later medieval and early modern period not only carefully studied the content of what Seneca, Cicero, and other ancient writers said (thus appropriating Stoicism and other ancient schools), but they also adopted their techniques of self-examination and self-improvement, albeit now with different technologies and new media.

Erasmus, for example, widely considered to be one of the greatest scholars of the Northern Renaissance, was a Christian humanist, independent scholar, and prolific writer who "embraced the humanistic belief in an individual's capacity for self-improvement."[13] He argued for reading the ancients texts in their original language and promoted education. Children should be educated to fulfill their potential as rational beings. He also recommended studying the classic Greek and Latin texts (for example Cicero) next to the Bible and the Church Fathers. With regard to self-development, he advised the development of inner qualities. Influenced by the Stoics, he stressed the importance of developing the soul and the pleasures of the spirit. Erasmus's fool in *The Praise of Folly* mocks the world. Self-improvement is important in a world of political and clerical corruption.

But Erasmus's work, success, and influence in the sixteenth century is unthinkable without the invention of the printing press by Johannes Gutenberg in the previous century—and about five hundred years earlier in China. Gutenberg's invention of mechanical movable type printing, using his knowledge of metals as a goldsmith, enabled mass communication between the scholars of the Renaissance and established academic communities across European borders. Erasmus and his Reformation rival Luther were bestselling authors, and their ideas could now easily spread outside the immediate grip of religious and political authorities. The technological revolution of the printing press was not only an academic development but also a societal and political one.

The printing press also created new readers. Whereas first reading and writing was reserved for a small elite of monks and intellectuals, the invention of the printing press opened up the circle of the selected few to an ever-wider circle of literate people, until in the twentieth century the masses started reading. Usually, the story then ends with lamenting the invention of digital technologies, notably the internet, which are supposed to have ended this old culture of humanism. Like other pessimistic humanists, Sloterdijk thinks that humanism is banished to the archives. I disagree. Quite the oppose has happened: digital technologies are continuing the ancient and humanist traditions, albeit in a different medium and supported by different technologies. It may well be true that people read fewer books, although that medium continues to attract many. But they read and write online, and partly they do so in order to continue the practices of self-examination and self-improvement—in the West started by the ancient Greek sages and Roman writers and transformed into practices of verbalization and confession by bishops and saints. On social media, in particular, people explore themselves, present an ideal self they try to attain, and confess their stories of self-improvement. To put it bluntly: in a Catholic spirit, they confess their sins. In a Protestant spirit, they show to the community of self-improvers the success they have attained. And like Erasmus, they use the new mass media and technologies to create new communities. Never before were there so many humanist writers and readers.

Of course, this new form of digital humanism is not completely the same as in the Renaissance or in the Reformation, let alone in ancient times. It is thoroughly transformed by modernity. And modernity in this context means individualism and a growing obsession with oneself as a unique individual. The self-care of the ancients, the confessions of Augustine, and the Renaissance building of the *humanitas*—let alone the Buddhist practices—were not about creating individual unique selves. Augustine began his *Confessions* with "Great art Thou, O Lord," and pages of praise follow before it gets to personal stories about his childhood—which again involve God in every sentence. This radically changes in modern times. When Rousseau writes his *Confessions*, it is about himself and him alone.[14] It starts with the words, "the man I shall portray will be myself. Simply myself. I know my own heart and understand my fellow man. But I am made unlike any one I have ever met." This unique self he puts on display in his book, and it has to be an authentic, true self: "I have displayed myself as I was, as vile and despicable when my behavior was such, as good, generous, and noble when I was so."[15]

Today people put their own "unique" and "authentic" self on display on social media. They show themselves "as they are." They share their stories. All this happens in a new medium. But their confessions without priests and without God are still aimed at self-examination and self-improvement. Together with the apps that enable us to measure our progress, we are still engaged in the business of knowing and improving ourselves. We write to friends. We are part of what Marshall McLuhan called *The Gutenberg Galaxy*: the printing press had a huge influence on European culture and consciousness.[16] Like Rousseau, we post and say: "So let the numberless legion of my fellow men gather around me, and hear my confessions. Let them groan at my depravities, and blush for my misdeeds. But let each one of them reveal his heart at the foot of Thy throne with equal sincerity."[17] Everyone is supposed to put their unique and authentic selves on display, fully transparent, with the purpose of knowledge and improvement.

Yet the nature of self-knowledge and self-examination has changed because the technology and the medium have changed. Text is largely replaced by images, and quantitative knowledge is privileged. We measure and compare by means of images and numbers. And we do not put our personal stories at the foot of God's throne, but at the feet of our "friends" and "followers." This sharing and comparing creates mental suffering. We are restless, worried, and anxious. What will they think of me? How will they judge me? Did I self-improve enough? What is my image (Latin: *imago*) in the perception of others?

To understand these troubles, we may again turn to Rousseau, who wrote in *Emile* about self-love and *amour-propre*: whereas it is natural to love oneself and try to preserve oneself, once we compare ourselves to others, things go wrong. We are no longer content, and we become jealous, deceitful, vain, and wicked.[18] Rousseau thought that we are good by nature, but corrupted by society. In society, people conceive new needs and become subject to the empire of opinion, "basing their own existence on the judgments of others."[19] Social media create such a modern society where opinion reigns. The "they" or "one" (see also Heidegger: *das man*) is put on the throne. This has transformed the initially humanist culture into a toxic variant, one that makes people unhappy and drives some into the arms of death. Quantified, datafied, and with our body and soul naked on display, we are continuously compared, categorized, and evaluated. Our humanist "friends" turn into our competitors and enemies. Like Rousseau, we become vulnerable to paranoia. Evaluations end in self-loathing. It is a race we can never win: we are always losers. Our confessions are analyzed and the evaluation is clear and always the same: it is not enough. We are not good enough.

In the meantime, the corporate data shepherds count their profits. An eternally unsatisfied consumer—the absolute horror, according to Buddhist teaching—is an ideal target for advertising. People obsessed with self-care in the mode of amour-propre are ideal cattle in the data economy. They continue to produce data and are open to personalized advertising, which, by connecting to the secrets of people's hearts just shared with thousands of "friends" and by taking advantage of their taste for competition, produces new needs and makes the owners of the new technologies and media richer than they already are. In the meantime, this perverse form of post-Christian confession and neohumanistic communication produces subjects that continuously fail and lose, until their tortured bodies and minds give up. The combination of self-improvement culture and the pressure to achieve as an individual is lethal. A point comes when we have to give up. As Byung-Chul Han puts it in *The Burnout Society*: "the achievement-subject is no longer able to be able."[20]

But in contrast to what neo-Stoic, post-Protestant, and neoliberal culture tries to tell us, it's not just our fault if we fail. It's not just our individual responsibility to improve things. We should also pay attention to the social and cultural environment that turns us into self-obsessed and eternally unhappy self-improvers: modern society.

3

The Society

Modern Self-Obsession from Rousseau
to Hipster Existentialism

Jean-Jacques Rousseau's turn to his own, individual self
was the beginning of a story of modern self-obsession
and individualism that continues to this day. Psychologi-
cally, being too self-centered and socially isolated is dangerous. Émile Durkheim, one of the founding figures of
sociology, argued that it can lead to death, in particular
suicide. He called this "egoistic suicide." However, contrary to what the term may suggest, he didn't think that
suicide was a personal matter and that individuals were to
blame; instead, he argued that the lack of social integration and solidarity was the problem. Our obsession with
self-improvement is not just an individual but also and
mainly a societal problem, which requires solutions at the
societal level.

Yet the psychological approach is a good starting point
to think through these issues. Durkheim was not the first
to see a connection between self-obsession and death. It is
a theme that has always been known in Western culture

under the name of *narcissism*, which in modern times found its way to psychology from Freud's paper *On Narcissism* to the *Diagnostic and Statistical Manual of Mental Disorders*, a handbook used by contemporary psychiatrists, which lists "narcissistic personality disorder": a pathological overestimation of one's abilities and an excessive need for admiration and affirmation.[1] Rousseau himself was already well aware of the dangers of narcissism: a healthy self-love is fine, but not what he called *amour-propre*. In his 1752 comedy *Narcissus, or the Lover of Himself*, a man falls in love with a painting of himself dressed as a woman. He sees his mistake and all ends well, and the value of loving one another is confirmed.

The ancient Greek myth of Narcissus, told in Ovid's *Metamorphoses*, ends less well. It tells the story of Echo and Narcissus. Echo, a mountain nymph, falls in love with the handsome Narcissus, who was walking in the woods. Narcissus rejects her and is punished by Nemesis, the goddess of revenge. She lures him to a pool where he sees himself. Narcissus, not knowing it is merely his own reflection, falls in love with the image of himself. But the love cannot be returned, and he dies (in some versions, he commits suicide). The myth is often used to point to "narcissism" and self-obsession as a psychological and societal problem. But trying to know yourself and improve yourself are not themselves problematic; they become problematic when they go together with self-obsession and individualistic competition, as Rousseau pointed out. His analysis, in the preface to *Narcissus* and elsewhere, goes beyond an individualistic diagnosis: the problem is a society in which people compare themselves to others and try to distinguish themselves. Rousseau and Durkheim agree that the root of the problem of narcissism is to be found in our relations to others and in modern society, rather than in the individual alone. Paradoxically, our self-obsession is a social problem.

Moreover, through contemporary social media people become even more obsessed with their own *image*, that is, the way they appear to themselves and to others. This fixation on self and self-image means we are no longer open to the other, and in the absence of true relationality (rather than amour-propre with its comparison to others) and empathy we risk fading away. If Narcissus really knew himself, as the ancient philosophical maxim demands, he would have known that this was merely the reflection of himself, and that such a kind of self-love leads nowhere. Narcissus was so busy exercising the wrong kind of self-love that he not only ignored Echo's suffering but also lost his natural self-love in the form of the instinct of self-preservation. The message for today is clear: self-improvement in the form of self-obsession leads nowhere and eventually to death. And if the current technologies boost this wrong kind of self-love, then we have a problem. If our screens become mirrors for our narcissistic self, we miss the chance for empathic engagement with others and an openness for the world around us: a nondestructive and much better form of self-improvement.

In *Alone Together*, psychoanalyst and MIT professor Sherry Turkle argues that if we are distracted by our phones, we do pay not enough attention to one another. And robots do not offer empathy; instead, these "relational artifacts" open up "new possibilities for narcissistic experience," which sees other people as part of the self (what psycho-analyst Heinz Kohut calls *selfobjects*) or as objects. Instead, we need genuine relationships with real people. The same can be said of social media, where people perform their "better self" and anxiously confess their secrets but feel at the same time that they *have* to. We are too self-obsessed, the networks encourage narcissism: not only love of self, but also "a personality so fragile that it needs constant support." For this, real people are not needed: "made-to-measure representations" suffice. Real people can hardly be handled: some people even avoid direct contact with others. Turkle reports that even phone calls are sometimes already perceived as threatening. They are not only con-straining since unsuitable for multitasking, but they are also too direct. Too much exposure, too much is revealed. Too awkward, weird. Others are a problem, something to be controlled and managed. Our current technoculture encourages "narcissistic ways of relating to the world."[2]

At a time when the full power of digital social media had not yet emerged, American psychologists Jean Twenge and Keith Campbell already observed a rise in narcissism and spoke of a "narcissism epidemic" in which people focus on themselves and have unrealistic expectations about themselves, which makes them depressed. The internet and celebrity culture play a role in creating an environment that stimulates this narcissism. The authors write: "The Internet allows people to present an inflated and self-focused view of themselves to the world, and encourages them to spend hours each day contemplating their images."[3] They also call it a "Look at me!" mentality.[4] (Or, in the words of Twenge's first book, "generation me.") People feel entitled, special, and unique. Faced with recession and a highly competitive world, this generation faces a huge tension between expectations and reality. Today's social media do not help. But there is also a problem with education. Parents and teachers boost self-esteem and stress how special we are. Confidence is good, but overconfidence and self-admiration are problematic. The authors seem to agree with the advice of the grandmothers they interviewed who, against the view of mothers who thought that one cannot have too much self-esteem, insisted on the dangers: "overly high self-esteem" leads to people who are "arrogant, self-centered, selfish, and spoiled."[5]

Even spiritual practices, which have the potential to take us out of ourselves and cultivate compassion toward others, can—at least in the West—lead to what Scott Kaufman calls "spiritual narcissism." Studies have shown that spiritual practices such as yoga and meditation that aim to quiet the ego often do the opposite: they boost self-centrality. People feel that they know more than others and esteem themselves so highly that they acquire a sense of superiority. Instead of transcending the ego and opening the mind, these ancient spiritual techniques are used in the service of the ego and self-enhancement.[6] Spiritual self-improvement is then an illusion, and again we end up with arrogant, narcissistic individuals.

This criticism is not new. Modern Western society has long been criticized for its individualism. For example, in the early nineteenth century Alexis de Tocqueville observed American people withdrawing from society. And in the 1970s, before the popularization of digital technologies and in the time of TV, historian Christopher Lasch already

29

spoke of a "culture of narcissism" and pointed to the fascination with fame and the fear of competition, but also to the political and spiritual movements of the 1960s and 1970s.[7] In an article in the *New York Review of Books*, published some years before his bestseller, he writes about a generation of Americans that turned away from politics and instead embraced either religion or a cult of personal growth:

> Having no hope of improving their lives in any of the ways that matter, people have convinced themselves that what matters is psychic self-improvement: getting in touch with their feelings, eating health food, taking lessons in ballet or belly dancing, immersing themselves in the wisdom of the East, jogging, learning how to "relate," overcoming the "fear of pleasure." Harmless in themselves, these pursuits, elevated to a program and wrapped in the rhetoric of "authenticity" and "awareness," signify a retreat from the political turmoil of the recent past. Indeed Americans seem to wish to forget not only the Sixties, the riots, the New Left, the disruptions on college campuses, Vietnam, Watergate, and the Nixon presidency, but their entire collective past.[8]

Lasch's criticism is sometimes interpreted as conservative and connected to Allan Bloom's complaints about the self-centeredness of the youth, but the opposite could also be argued: Lasch's book expresses the disappointment of a neo-Marxist, who sees how the revolution has been abandoned for the cult of self-improvement.[9] As a cultural historian, he has a point: if we want to understand why millennials are narcissistic, we have to study those who created their narcissism, namely their parents, the boomers. To understand our contemporary self-obsession, I propose to go back half a century and look at the 1960s–1970s counterculture and its flirtation with the new technologies, a counterculture that became as mainstream and pervasive as the technologies it embraced.

HIPPIES IN CYBERSPACE

Although hippies proclaimed that they wanted to make the world a better place, this has remained the dream about which John Lennon sang. In practice, the baby-boom generation created a highly individualistic and competitive society and engaged in the rampant consumerism criticized by Lasch. Those who carried on the ancient tradition of "knowing yourself" and self-perfection did so in a way that, like the ancient Stoics and Christian monks, turned away from a society that became increasingly unlivable and a planet that became much less hospitable to humans than ever before. Influenced by modern self-obsession, an entire generation started to work on themselves—and, luckily for the flourishing self-improvement industry, they have not finished. Lifelong learning and lifelong self-improvement became the motto. For this purpose, they looked beyond the Western tradition, appropriated Eastern practices, and reimagined all kinds of ancient rituals and healing methods. As in the Dark Ages, spiritual self-enhancement and stoical withdrawal seemed the only remaining road to happiness in the hellhole of neoliberalist capitalism they helped to sustain in their day jobs. Self-improvement, rather than social change, was and is the motto of this generation. After the drugs came the books, workshops, retreats, and New Age accouterments that were used to work on the self.

But their most powerful self-improvement machine had yet to be built: the internet. In Silicon Valley, something extraordinary happened during the 1980s and 1990s: Californian hippiedom met high tech and produced a terrifyingly attractive offspring that can best be described as a combination of hippie self-improvement ideas and digital technologies such as the personal computer, the internet, and later the mobile phone and the smartphone that would soon dominate our lives. As Fred Turner has written, people from the counterculture became interested not only in rock music, LSD, and Eastern religions but also in technology.[10] No longer merely an instrument of the military-industrial complex, computing became a tool for change, social and personal. Steve Jobs is a case in point: when he was young, he practiced Zen Buddhism and took LSD, but he also worked with Steve Wozniak on what would become known as the Mac. This work on technologies was meant to change the world and change the self. The personal computing revolution was a new step on to road to self-improvement. Apple's original mission statement was "the empowerment of man" and "to help change the way we think, work, learn, and communicate."[11] In 1980 Jobs called computers "tools for the mind."[12] Later the internet became a tool for the exploration of a new world: cyberspace. Ex-hippies started roaming cyberspace in search of personal liberation. First meant as tools to change the world, computers and the internet became tools for self-improvement—and for making money.

However, this surprising combination of a romantic counterculture and high tech also boosted, and continues to boost, all the problematic aspects of modern self-improvement culture.[13] The next generations became even more obsessed with themselves and with improving themselves. They did everything to perform better: workouts and yoga (a heritage of the hippies), but also taking pills (Ritalin, for example), going to therapy, and using all kinds of apps to learn new skills and work on themselves. Since Freud it is not only important to work on the self that is known, as the ancients and the humanist did; it is also a requirement to find out about your *unconscious* issues. Therapy became a must, first in California (again), then in the rest of the world. Those who do not go to therapy are seen as lazy: they refuse to properly work on themselves. You owe it to your partner, your parents, your friends, and the people around you to constantly try to improve yourself. Most important, you owe it to yourself. Forget about changing the world. Like the Stoics, you better focus on improving yourself. You should take care of yourself, using the techniques, therapies, and technologies available.

In her book *In Therapy We Trust*, Eva Moskowitz sees an age obsessed with emotional well-being and a belief in therapy.[14] Psychotherapy replaces prayer. We worship the psyche and its priests. Feelings are seen as sacred and need to be managed. We are preoccupied with trying to be happy. Treatments are offered. Like self-improvement in general, the mental health industry is growing fast. Psychologists and psychiatrists, but also all kinds of therapists and counselors. And if that is too tiresome, simple and quick solutions are preferred: pills such as antidepressants. The historical background? Individualism, consumer culture, the decline of religion, the rise of the mass media, war, and the image of the unhappy housewife. Moskowitz also points to the promotion of emotional honesty in the 1970s and later the confession of psychological sins. She gives the example of *The Oprah Winfrey Show*, a TV talk show that aired across several decades and that had self-disclosure and self-improvement advice among its key ingredients.

But that was only the beginning. TV focused on celebrities and only gradually started to expand its attention to ordinary people. This changed radically with the internet, and especially with digital social media. Today the masses display their emotional struggles on Facebook, YouTube, TikTok, and other platforms. Confessing in the name of emotional honesty and admitting your vulnerabilities is now done publicly and by everyone, not just celebrities. Emotional struggles are *shared*. The management and display of emotions and mental problems is mediated by platforms and apps. Therapy is no longer limited to the couch of the psychotherapist: social media communication has itself become part of the culture of self-disclosure, self-knowledge, and self-improvement. What was once seen as belonging to the secrets of the troubled soul—meant only for God and his mediators or for the therapist—is now open and accessible to (almost) anyone. Self-improvement advice is not only given by professionals but also by "friends" on social media. All opinions are welcome. We are all little celebrities who do our own stripteases of the emotional mind while hundreds or thousands of Oprahs watch and comment. Improve yourself and show your success and failures. Failing hard is okay, as long as you share—and take your pills.

HIPSTER EXISTENTIALISM

In addition to these influences and practices, the current self-improvement culture takes the form of a consumerist hipster culture that, buying and selling all kinds of products that are supposed to lead to self-improvement and change (social change, environmental change), not only contributes to the gross national product by commodifying the counterculture of the parents but is also indirectly influenced by another set of ideas inherited from the 1960s: existentialism.

Philosophical existentialism has a long history, but it became popular and a mass product through the work of the French philosopher Jean-Paul Sartre. In his 1946 lecture *Existentialism Is a Humanism*, Sartre defines the first principle of existentialism: "Man is nothing other than what he makes of himself."[15] Or, put in philosophical jargon: you don't have an essence, you exist. You are not a thing but a project. Sartre argued that humans are not objects with an essence, like cauliflowers or a piece of garbage; we are subjects and project ourselves in the future. Design yourself and your life. Be free! Or, in the feminist version promoted by his partner Simone de Beauvoir in her book *The Second Sex*, "One is not born but becomes a woman."[16] Gender, like the self, is constructed. We are what we make of ourselves, and her message is: women, don't let yourself be made and defined by men.

As the title of his book says, Sartre puts his existentialism in the tradition of humanism. But an important difference with historical forms of humanisms is that there is no longer a "human nature in which I can place my trust."[17] It is up to me how I define myself—my own, unique self. It is a modern, individualist version of humanism that rejects tradition. But like historical humanisms, Sartre's existentialism is all about the active shaping and making of your own self. As Olivia Goldhill puts it, "Sartre was the original self-help guru."[18] In the 1960s, an entire generation was influenced by his existentialism (and that of his partner). It has been adopted, once more, by today's self-improvement culture. And that culture is demanding, also in its consumerism. The simple existentialist coffee is no longer sufficient; it has to be a special one. Authentic selves need authentic products. But these are details. Work is to be done, and it's work on the self. And that's not so easy, and in any case much less easy than ordering the right kind of coffee or getting a dog that suits your personality. The freedom to define yourself, so much struggled for by previous generation(s), has also become a burden.

Fyodor Dostoyevsky, who influenced Sartre, already saw this clearly. In *The Brothers Karamazov* and *Notes from Underground*, he pointed out that individual freedom and choice are hard to bear. Freedom produces suffering. The American philosopher Marjorie Grene called her introduction to existentialism, published not long after Sartre's lecture, *Dreadful Freedom*. And this is also our predicament in today's self-improvement culture: having rejected tradition, we are "condemned to be free,"[19] as Sartre said, not only in the sense that we have to make moral choices, on which Dostoevsky and Sartre focused, but also in the sense that we are condemned to work on ourselves. Not to do that would be "bad faith," to use a term from Sartre. It would deny our existential freedom.

Another term that was paramount in existentialism, which is still very important today in our self-improvement culture, is "authenticity." Rousseau already stressed the value of authenticity in his work. But what is authenticity? Apart from the consideration that people might not want to see your true self—as psychologist Adam Grant put it, "We all have thoughts and feelings that we believe are fundamental to our lives, but that are better left unspoken"[20]—it is not clear where and how this authentic or "true" self is to be found. Often, for example in Rousseau, the notion of authenticity is linked to the assumption that there is some kind of internal, private space to which we have privileged access.[21] Perhaps we have a kind of "essence," something that is our own and not dependent on the external world. But how do I know that essence? Is it good? Does it even exist? Existentialists such as Kierkegaard, Heidegger, and Sartre have their own solution to this problem: we do not have an essence, but we exist. We have to become what we are, to use Kierkegaard's phrase. Heidegger and Sartre think that we always project ourselves into the future. We are not an object. What we are is always at issue, always in question. Sartre's concept of authenticity is linked to his view of freedom: being authentic is not being determined by what is given, by our "facticity." We constitute ourselves through our choices.[22] Of course there are constraints. But, radicalizing the Stoics, Sartre thinks that all depends on our own interpretations and commitments. How significant the constraints are is up to us. We have to accept that responsibility for becoming ourselves and that radical freedom.

Others have also criticized the idea of an inner, hidden, and fixed authentic self. Freud already questioned a self that is totally transparent to us. As we have seen, Michel Foucault thinks that the self is a work of art. He agrees with the existentialists that we constitute ourselves. We can choose what kind of self we want to be. Moreover, according to a Buddhist doctrine, there is even no self. The self is an illusion.[23] (But let's stick with existentialism for now.)

The existentialist view that it is our own freedom and responsibility what we make of ourselves is a powerful idea that opens up a lot of philosophical space for an active, if not aggressive, self-improvement culture. A culture that is humanist but also partly (post)humanist already, since the idea of a fixed or original authentic self is abandoned. Unlike Rousseau and after Freud, in late modern times we no longer have the comfort of returning to the home-self, our inner self that we feel at home with. That self is radically questioned and sometimes annihilated. If we want to improve ourselves, we have to make that self and accept its instability. One could say that the self is unhomely (German: *unheimlich*). We cannot fully know it and we cannot get a full grip on it. It is not even a thing. Yet, at the same time, we are asked to improve it. We inherited from the existentialists the task to make ourselves, but we also still use the language of construction and production, which seems to posit the self as a thing. And it is unclear how a stable self can be created once it has been radically destabilized.

There are alternative interpretations of authenticity that do not lead to individualism, self-absorption, and self-indulgence. For example, Charles Taylor has proposed one that is about self-transcendence: an inward turn that takes us beyond the self.[24] Maybe going beyond the self is the solution. However, that's for later. Let's first further explore the direct line from the hippies and the existentialists to our contemporary idea that we need to work on ourselves.

Today we continue this existentialist-humanist culture focused on the self and its authenticity, including its conundrums. But now we use different technologies and media than Sartre and his historical predecessors. Reading and writing novels, as Sartre did, is at least partly superseded by practices around digital technologies. Social media, blogs, videos, and websites provide building sites for the unique projects that we are supposed to define: ourselves. The silent dialogues and slow humanist self-development that took place during the writing and reading of books have been replaced by the loud, screaming, and fast images of selves that desperately try to be born. Or rather: selves that are under construction and need regular updates. There is no time for self-development. Self-improvement is a project, and it needs to be managed, measured, and lead to outcomes. The self needs to be performed: every day, every hour, and preferably every minute. We click and browse as if our lives—and selves!—depend on it.

Yet existentialist self-makers do not only do their work by using humanist technologies such as books or posthumanist technologies such as social media; they also buy products and services for self-improvement. They do not make themselves without help. They do their duty as consumers: they buy books, workshop participation, courses, and so on. The fact that, in some cases, it concerns a market and service for a specific subculture (for example, hipster culture) does not change the nature of that consumerism. True existentialists would balk at this. In a neoliberal context, existentialist authentic choice is replaced by consumer choice. The message that we should make ourselves and be authentic is translated by advertising and marketing into the demand that we buy "authentic" products. This is what existentialists call bad faith. This is not the kind of choice we should be making. The ideas of the hippies and the existentialists, however well meant they may have been and whatever value there may be in them, are commodified and abused. The ideas of the poets and writers of the 1960s become goods and services that can be monetized, bought, and sold. And we are commodified in the process. We are not treated as humans that exist but as things, objects, products. Moreover, we are instruments of others who benefit from our self-improvement work.

The self-workers are not the only stakeholders in these practices and technologies of the self. Some people make money from all these (post)humanist efforts to create a better self. In order to understand why contemporary self-improvement culture is so persistent, even if it has all these problematic aspects, let's take a closer look at its socioeconomic dimension, in particular its political economy.

4

The Political Economy

Self-Taming and Exploitation Under
Wellness Capitalism

The philosophies of Plato and Aristotle educated the rich youth, the nobles, the kings, and the emperors. Socrates was teaching young wealthy and powerful men how to improve their souls. Plato was of noble birth and believed that aristocracy was the best form of government. Aristotle tutored Alexander the Great, king of Macedonia and conqueror of an empire that stretched from Egypt to India. As Hannah Arendt shows in *The Human Condition*, political freedom in ancient Greece was reserved for those who did not have to work or labor. Consequently, the philosophies developed were usually taught to, and sometimes meant only for, these free men. (Socrates proposed to include women in the guardian class and acknowledged that he learned from Diotima, but women did not participate in the Platonic dialogues; Socrates was socializing with young men.)

But this changed in Hellenistic and Roman times. Marcus Aurelius was an emperor, and Seneca addressed his letters to Lucilius, the governor of Sicily. But the Stoic philosopher Epictetus, who influenced Seneca and whom we encountered in chapter 2, was born a slave. His name means "acquired." He was treated as property. Before he obtained his freedom, he was a slave in Rome to a wealthy man who was secretary to Nero. Unsurprisingly, therefore, he advocated a philosophy that turns inward to the self. If you cannot change the world around you, forget about it, bracket it, don't care about it. It doesn't matter that you are not free, a slave, imprisoned. You do not even possess things, but that's okay; you should not be attached to external things anyway. Focus on yourself and try to improve your soul. You have a master and are not free in that external sense, but you can learn to master yourself. That freedom of the soul is real freedom. If you attain this kind of freedom, you are truly free and all the others, even the so-called masters and emperors, are in fact slaves if they are not masters of themselves. In other words: an ideal philosophy for slaves, prisoners, or anyone else who is not free or feels not free. And since it does not really question the basic structure of society, it supports those who benefit from slavery and other forms of oppression and hegemony.

In Renaissance humanist times, Erasmus mocked the corrupt practices in the Roman Catholic Church and turned down offers to advance in the curia, the administration of the Holy See. But he neither rejected the Catholic faith itself nor the political power of the Church. Martin Luther challenged those, of course, and in this way had considerable political influence: the Reformation followed, which was not only a religious but also a political revolution. Yet all this was not meant to fundamentally change the order of feudal society. At most, Protestantism would eventually contribute to the birth of another hegemonic order, capitalism (see again Max Weber's argument). Writing and reading books *can* be politically dangerous, and Luther is often seen as a revolutionary, but neither humanists nor their books were so dangerous for the existing social order that they radically overturned it. Not everyone could read, the more individualist approach promoted by Luther and his followers in the next centuries did not always lead to collective action, and the intellectual elite formed by the medium of the book and the printing technology did not really challenge the power of its kings and princes. On the contrary, sometimes they explicitly supported it. In Florence, Niccolò Machiavelli writes in his *The Prince*, an instruction manual for new princes and royals, that the success of their rule can justify the use of immoral means to achieve this. Cruel deeds and deceit are acceptable if that secures the prince's power. Make sure you are feared; that fear maintains your power. Very different from Erasmus's belief in a virtuous noble ruler, and—needless to say—highly influential among the royalty of the time.

Book-oriented humanism also came in handy for the capitalists of industrial societies. Books helped to keep people disciplined. Books were education, but also, as Peter Sloterdijk has suggested, a form of taming—more specifically: self-taming.[1] If humans are indeed what Sloterdijk calls "self-shepherding creatures" (not just herd creatures, as Nietzsche argued), then this is very useful for those in power. It is good that people read in their free time. It means that when they come to work, they are already self-disciplined sheep who can be exploited. Busy with reading and with working on themselves, self-shepherding humanist workers and shepherding managers will not question the socioeconomic order of society. Workers can be disciplined and fenced in the zoo of the workplace because they have already self-disciplined through education and have fenced themselves in by means of humanist technologies and practices such as reading, sitting, and other forms of taming and self-taming. With Sloterdijk and Nietzsche, one could say that humanist readers turn themselves into "friendly, loyal dogs." Self-improvement thus means here becoming a good, docile dog. In *Twilight of the Idols* Nietzsche says of improvement,

> To call the taming of an animal its "improvement" sounds almost like a joke to our ears. Anyone who knows what happens in menageries has doubts about whether any beast gets "improved" there. The beast gets weakened, it is made less dangerous, and through the depressing feeling of fear, through pain, through wounds and hunger, it becomes a sickly beast. It is no different with the tamed human being.[2]

In Thus Spoke Zarathustra, Nietzsche posited his superhuman (*Übermensch*) in opposition to this weakened, tamed beast: an aristocratic and life-affirming more-than-human. Karl Marx, however, had another view of self-improvement and the kind of society that should accompany it. He also saw the suffering of humankind, especially the suffering of workers. Of course we need improvement and self-improvement. But under the influence of Hegel, he argued that true self-realization is not something that you can do in your humanist or aristocratic leisure time; it is only possible through work, and more precisely work under conditions that are not capitalist, since capitalism precludes self-realization through its alienation and exploitation. In his *Economic and Philosophic Manuscripts of 1844*, Marx argued that people have to sell their labor in order to survive and cannot develop their human capacities. They become alienated from the product of their work, from the work, from human nature and themselves, from others. In this way they cannot realize themselves. Later Marx argued in *Capital* that workers do not get the surplus value they create with their labor: this value is taken by the capitalist. If we really want to improve ourselves and realize our humanity, therefore, we need to change the order of society. Capitalism, with its sickening alienation and exploitation, needs to end.

However, Marx could not foresee the rise of a form of capitalism that would go further than not paying people enough: a capitalism that would not pay people anything. And it would not only suck on the living labor of people working in industrial factories (to use Marx's vampire metaphor in *Capital*), but it would also target the self-improvement work people still tried to do in their so-called leisure time. Today, what Shoshana Zuboff calls "surveillance capitalism" feeds on the struggles of the human soul itself.[3] This includes the (post)humanist work on the self and self-improvement. Engaging with digital technologies, people not only work on themselves to improve themselves; *by doing this*, they also work for free for capitalists who use and sell their data, put them under surveillance, and manipulate them. Paradoxically, then, current capitalism does not so much threaten as stimulate self-improvement. It needs it in order to monetize it.

But for this system to work, the self needs first to be put under surveillance, datafied, and quantified.

WELLNESS CAPITALISM AND THE SELF-IMPROVEMENT INDUSTRY

When it comes to making a profit from people's efforts at self-improvement, the first thing that comes to mind is the industry of books, workshops, courses, therapies, and treatments that have mushroomed in the past decades. This goes together with a turn in capitalist economies to the personal "needs" of body and mind. Business has since long discovered that tired, depressed, anxious, and spiritually empty workers and consumers are fair game for new products and services that claim to offer "wellness." Partly this is about the creation of false needs, as Herbert Marcuse already argued in the 1960s,[4] but it also answers to a real phenomenon: people are really tired and burned-out from life and work in modern capitalist society. The answer of the industry has been: relax, we can offer you products and services that make you feel better again. Wellness capitalism was born. The global wellness economy is currently valued at USD 4.5 trillion.[5] Beauty salons, anti-aging treatments, nutrition, advice, weight loss treatments, fitness, traditional and alternative medicine, spa treatments, and wellness tourism are meant to make people feel less bad after spending long hours in front of their screens or on long delivery shifts. In this way, capitalism exploits people doubly: first as workers who try to improve their performance during working hours, then as consumers of "wellness" during their leisure time, when they try to recover from the work.

But it does not stop at relaxation and wellness. In addition, self-improvement is again the mantra: relax by buying our products and services, but also work on yourself and buy our advice. If you are tired, depressed, burned-out, anxious, and so on, it's because you don't lead your life in the right way. Time to hack your life, time to improve yourself. Watch this video, buy this book, register for this retreat, listen to this podcast. As I said in the introduction: the idea is that you're not good enough. Self-improvement and self-help techniques are there to get you through life and improve it. You thought that you are good enough as you are? How dare you! Get started, move it. Improve yourself! Our coaches, apps, self-help books, motivational speakers, institutes, travel packages, and spiritual programs are here to help you.

Women are especially targeted. In the United States, 70 percent of self-help customers are women. The traditional demographic for self-help products was middle-aged women and boomers now in their sixties and seventies.[6] But millennials have joined the boomers to form a ready and willing market for self-improvement, and young men are now also self-improving as if their life depends on it. In 2015, 94 percent of millennials reported making personal improvement commitments and spending almost twice as much on it as boomers (almost $300 per month), while their average income was half as much.[7] The industry is working hard to keep them addicted. Millennials are now driving the growth of the American self-improvement industry, which is estimated to grow to more than $13 billion by 2022. An illustration of where the investment goes: when Prince Harry got a job in March 2021, he didn't go into finance or art business. He joined a billion-dollar Silicon Valley unicorn startup that does personal development coaching. The firm claims to help people to "reach their best self,"[8] thereby completely resonating with millennials and Generation Z. Mental health and self-improvement are hot.

Technology assists all these wellness and self-improvement practices. Self-help apps are used to learn language, code, mediate and fall asleep, workout, cook, and so on. You want to relax? You want to improve yourself? There is an app for that. The app helps you to cope with stress and anxiety. You can use an app to workout, do yoga, follow a diet. Or try a Tik Tok video, a meditation podcast, or—if you're old-fashioned or *really* alternative—read a book. Meditation app firms Headspace and Calm saw their revenue soar. The economic crisis influenced people's mood. And during the coronavirus pandemic the digital self-improvement and self-help industry was "having a moment," as Hester Bates put it.[9] After the initial "slob out" in the couch (say, binge watching Netflix), people started to want to use the time to improve themselves. When the outer world closed down and was a frightening place, it was time for an inward turn. The self-improvement industry benefits from that monetized form of neo-Stoicism and is bigger than ever, thereby helped and amplified by social media and by American culture with its myth of the self-made man and its obsession with personal growth: "There is nothing about you or your life that cannot be enhanced, monetized, upgraded, or learned from."[10] Using the lockdown as an opportunity for self-improvement was not only desired but also expected. Social media "friends" and apps were watching to see if you made good use of your time.

But while these wellness treatments and self-improvement work may enable people to mentally survive under precarious circumstances, they do not make them happier. On the contrary. As already suggested, the culture of self-improvement can lead to psychological problems and even suicide. But both self-improvement and these psychological problems also have a political, socioeconomic, and ideological aspect: they support, and are even promoted by, a neoliberal and capitalist system that lives on our unhappiness and channels our attention to individual self-help and self-improvement as opposed to social change. In neoliberal societies, in which the state provides minimal welfare and health care and supports highly competitive employment markets, people are forced to be self-reliant and are encouraged to view themselves as commodities. Self-improvement is then a capitalist imperative. It becomes a means of profit making itself and puts people under further pressure. Social change remains out of view, and capitalists benefit from this. As Bryce Gordon summarizes Marxist research on this topic, the current rise in rates of depression and anxiety are not just a psychological problem but are also connected with self-improvement and self-care trends, which appeal to internet-engaged millennials and have as their foundation "a flawed, individualist approach to problems that are collective in nature."[11]

Here another demographic comes into view, which is not liberal, female, and hipster, but conservative, male, and career-oriented. Gordon tells of young, right-wing men who embrace values such as masculinity, earning money, starting a family, and taking care of yourself by therapy and adjusting your habits while accepting the existing power hierarchies and capitalism. But young women also spend their limited discretionary income on self-improvement and self-care. In the end, all demographics support a consumerist, capitalist version of self-improvement culture. They have to, in order to survive. But it is not only a way of *coping* with capitalism; it is also *enabling* its prolongation and growth. This means that, once again, it becomes clear that the obsessive self-improvement culture and its implications are not just an individual problem. Yes, people are depressed and anxious. But individual solutions are not sufficient; a systemic solution is needed. Marxism claims to offer a way out. Gordon writes:

> The only effective way to address the rise in depression and anxiety is to end the economic order which places the vast majority of people in a tumultuous, insecure position, and build on in which human need is prioritized; that is, to end capitalism and build socialism. But that cannot be achieved through lifting weights or lighting candles, but only through unified collective action.[12]

By promoting the idea that we have to solve our problems only at the individual level, the self-improvement culture thus supports forms of capitalist exploitation and consumption, both at work and in our leisure time. In

addition, many people have precarious jobs. The unem-
ployed person has to be always stand-by for hiring, while
the employed person has to be ready to become unem-
ployed any time. *Both* categories of people engage in forms
of "self-improvement" that help to maintain the very system
and ideology that keep them in this dreadful position. Or
in Nietzschean language: we tame ourselves, and capitalism profits from it.

A telling example of what wellness capitalism does to
its workers is the "AmaZen box," introduced in May 2021 as
part of Amazon.com's WorkingWell program: a phonebooth-
like box put in the middle of an Amazon warehouse in
which overworked employees can go to watch mindfulness
and other mental health videos. As an article on the
"despair closet" has it, inside the box "nobody can hear you
scream."[13] The box has been heavily criticized. Instead of
improving wages and working conditions, workers are
offered a technological self-care solution that is unlikely to
address the real issue: the exploitation of the workers
under a capitalist system, which aggressively campaigns
against unionization and allegedly has its drivers pee in
water bottles. More generally, as Gordon Hull and Frank
Pasquale have argued,[14] U.S. employee wellness programs
provide an opportunity for employers to exercise increasing control over their employees and extend the workplace into the home and the bodies of workers. It also
makes individuals entirely responsible for their health in
the absence of public initiatives, and thus it contributes to
a further privatization and depoliticization of health and
wellness. Bad health is your own problem, not a public
matter.

51

Yet the rise of this self-help industry and wellness capitalism was not enough. Capitalism found a third way to generate profit from our problems and efforts at self-improvement: by collecting and selling our data. This data economy is not only a problem for privacy and other people's controlling our data, as Carissa Véliz has so clearly argued in her book *Privacy Is Power*. It is also a problem of capitalist exploitation. When we use social media and apps that help us with our self-improvement, we also produce content and data and in this way do what Christian Fuchs calls "digital labour"[15]: we work for the people who sell this content and data to advertisers. In this case, we do not get a (too) low wage for the value we generate, like workers in the nineteenth century or today in many parts of the world, even in so-called "advanced" countries such as the United States. No, we get nothing at all, zero. Self-improvement thus leads to a third way of exploitation. Moreover, in contrast to the other types of exploitation, which at least involve visible transactions, this data economy is usually hidden. We believe that we are working on ourselves, but actually we are making profit for tech companies and their clients.

AI is expected to amplify these problems, since through enhanced automation and the generation and analysis of large amounts of data, it further expands these possibilities for exploitation of workers not just at work, but also at home. Capitalist exploitation takes place not only in industrial contexts but has also entered the private sphere. We are data-producing cattle and are continuously tracked and monitored. This includes self-surveillance. No slave driver needed: we do it ourselves. The data technologies do not require the kind of surveillance that was common in the hospitals and prisons Foucault wrote about; by using all kinds of self-improvement apps, we track ourselves and keep records of our behavior. In a world twentieth-century intelligence services did not even dare to dream of, we put ourselves under 24/7 surveillance and meekly produce and upload our data to private corporations that monetize it.

Moreover, in contrast to the machines in the time of Marx, AI is a new exploitation machine that does not only touch our physical capacities but also works with our cognitive capacities and our emotions. It can increasingly do tasks such as "understanding" and writing texts, performing management and administration, "reading" emotional states, and so on. This enables manipulation and exploitation of humans in the workplace or outside of it, but also their replacement. In the context of private self-improvement, the coach and therapist are replaced by an app. Perhaps AI even makes humanity obsolete, an idea Nick Dyer-Witheford and colleagues mention in their book *Inhuman Power*, in which they critically engage with transhumanist accelerationist thinking. If current humans do no longer fit the technocapitalist system, then they need to be either enhanced or replaced by machines. If we cannot cope anymore, as is evident from our burnouts and depressions, then we are no longer needed. Then at best only technological self-improvement remains, the upgrading of people and the creation of a new type of human. Transhumanist technocapitalists are losing patience with the slow, humanist type of self-improvement. As we will see in the next chapter, they need cyborgs or robots. Dyer-Witheford and colleagues show that AI is now already an instrument of capital, leading to a concentration of wealth and power in the hands of the few.

The Nietzschean and especially the Marxist analysis thus suggests once more that we need to change the system rather than look for solutions only at an individual level. Yet the self-improvement culture tries to prevent us from thinking about society as a whole and encourages us to stick with individual solutions. One way it does that is by establishing self-improvement as a form of self-exploitation. Whereas in our day job we can still point to others who manage us and benefit from our work (although that is also changing; many people today are reluctantly self-employed or increasingly managed by machines), in the case of self-improvement it seems that we only have ourselves to blame when we exploit ourselves. What Byung-Chul Han says about the achievement society is also true for what we could call the self-improvement society: "The exploiter is simultaneously the exploit. Perpetrator and victim can no longer be distinguished."[16] We are the ones who wanted to improve ourselves. Any potential complaints, so it seems, are to be addressed to ourselves. By redefining exploitation as self-exploitation, the capitalist system remains unquestioned.

Moreover, while we are so busy with improving ourselves, the self we work on and our knowledge of that self are shaped in a very particular way, which is different from the self-knowledge and self-shaping that happened in humanist and earlier modern times: our self is not only put under surveillance but also *quantified*. The term "quantified self" refers to methods and technologies to collect and analyze personal data, for example about your health and sport activities. But we can also use it to define a specific way of knowing and shaping the self. Using our self-tracking devices and having ourselves scanned and categorized by algorithms when we are buying online, go through airport procedures, and register for events, we no longer come to know ourselves in terms of a complex character in a slow, ambiguous, multilayered story, as in a humanist letter or confessional novel. Instead, knowledge of ourselves is produced in terms of a collection of data, a digital profile, and numbers that show our performance. The question "Who am I?" no longer requires a painful and struggling writing or reading experience, as in humanist times; the question has been already answered by the algorithm. New technologies of the self are ready to tell us who we are, what we want, what we should know about ourselves, and, of course, how we can improve ourselves.

In the next chapter, I will further investigate how AI promotes new forms of self-knowledge and how AI may also be used to enable a very specific, technological form of self-improvement: self-enhancement. But let's first say more about the relation between technology and society.

TECHNOSOLUTIONISM AND CLASS SIGNALING

I have argued already that the current self-improvement culture tries to divert attention away from societal issues by focusing on individuals and their issues. A similar magic trick is going on when technological solutions are presented for complex societal problems. This is called *technosolutionism,* and it is endemic to Silicon Valley technoculture and to modern technoculture in general. A good example of this is the Hyperloop project developed by tech entrepreneur Elon Musk: a sealed tube with magnetic levitation and low air pressure through which a pod can travel with very little resistance and reach high speed.[17] Musk proposes the technology as a solution for traffic jams, for example between Los Angeles and San Francisco, but he ignores that transportation in California is a complex societal problem. Instead of analyzing the problem in all its complexity and considering other options (e.g., more public transportation, better traffic regulation, etc.), a technological solution is proposed: literally a shortcut.

In the context of self-improvement culture and the problems it raises, technosolutionism means that here too technological solutions are proposed—applied at individual level—without considering the societal complexity of the issues. A meditation app is supposed to solve anxiety; the societal conditions (such as precarious work conditions and fear mongering by mainstream media) that lead to anxiety are ignored. Individual enhancement of body and mind by means of pills and electronic devices is proposed instead of considering how our social environment (including our socioeconomic system, modern society, and youth culture) creates an environment in which people are under pressure to perform, to compete, to look good, to be perfect partners, and indeed to work on themselves. And like the self-taming and the self-exploitation already discussed, this is not some evil conspiracy: people themselves want, and believe in, these quick solutions, encouraged by the individualist and technosolutionist ideological environment they live in. To change society (for example, by collective action) and to really develop yourself in a slow, humanist kind of way are perceived as too demanding. A fast solution in the form of a technological shortcut is then very welcome. Self-improvement technologies are the hyperloop for dealing with a sick and unjust society.

Indeed, just as with the hyperloop, it's good to be aware of issues concerning equality and justice. This is a political and social problem in general, but self-improvement technologies also raise it. Not everyone has the time or the money to occupy themselves with self-improvement, and certainly not everyone has the time and money to get the technological solutions and fast-track their improvement. There could be (hidden?) forms of exclusion. And even if people are not excluded, it may well be that those who are already advantaged benefit more from the self-improvement technologies and techniques than others. Is self-improvement a privileged middle-class exercise? Or do different classes have different kinds of self-improvement technologies, perhaps to deal with different kinds of problems?

The first claim sounds plausible. In an article in which he compares contemporary elites with Victorians, Jason Tebbe argues that self-improvement is still a means for class signaling.[18] He shows that just as the nineteenth-century upper middle class was busy with *Bildung*, personal cultivation, and self-improvement by listening to music, learning languages, and making excursions (concert halls and nature were used as sites for improvement), today people display virtue and discipline in by means of fitness, yoga, organic food, and all kinds of forms of self-denial. Obesity is seen as a sign of moral failure; the lower classes cannot control themselves. And self-improvement requires money and time. Upper-class parents can send their children to expensive clubs, have time to support them with their *Bildung*, and have the money to prepare them for entry into a prestigious college. Working-class people are told that their poorer career prospects are their own fault. Self-improvement activities thus become "markers of bourgeois values" and a means to maintain social inequality. Self-improvement is a means of virtue signaling (inherited from Protestantism) and class signaling: "Look how well I'm doing and how much better I am than the rest." With intergenerational justice issues in mind, one could add: "I may not have it all, like the previous generation, but I'm self-improving!"

The same could be said about AI and self-improvement technologies, although here it might be interesting to differentiate them. As the second claim says, different classes may well (have to) use different technologies. For example, surveillance cameras for the lower classes, self-improvement apps for neo-Victorian hipsters. AI and other digital technologies are not just technologies of the self: they are also class technologies. And as self-improvement culture trickles down (without, however, the accompanying financial resources), this does not necessarily create equality: it may be the case that everyone self-improves, but some more than (and differently from) others. People of a privileged background can use the technology to empower themselves; others self-entertain and self-tame without really improving themselves or their social position. And human enhancement technologies may be available only to those who have the money to afford them. This creates a gap between the enhanced privileged and the unenhanced or less enhanced others.

However, the new, classy thing to do, reserved for the upper class and *not* for the middle class, is *not using technology at all*. If you are rich enough, you don't need to be on the internet all the time, deal with an endless list of emails, or struggle with a new app. You have people for that. You can literally afford to be offline. And, of course, at the same time you signal self-discipline and stoic nobility. You self-improve, but you can afford to talk to real people: real therapists, a personal training, a private physician, and so on. You can even read books. While the other classes are put under surveillance or need to rely on support from technology and feed surveillance capitalism, the new luxury is to self-improve offline and rely on personal service by humans. Relax, read, and chat! Not being hooked up to the net then offers an exclusive freedom only the 1 percent can enjoy. Being on the smartphone 24/7 is for the data-worker proletariat, the 99 percent.

In the next chapter, I will show how they are measured, quantified, and perhaps soon "enhanced" with the help of AI.

5

The Technology

Categorized, Measured, Quantified,
and Enhanced, or Why AI Knows Us
Better Than Ourselves

Contemporary digital technologies assist self-improvement in a number of ways. The most obvious one is that they inform: internet and social media inform us about books, apps, workshops, and all kind of methods of self-improvement. But as we have seen, they also do more than that: the technologies compare us to others. We see how well others are doing, and we want to improve ourselves. Companies are interested in that to target us with advertising and sell products and services.

Let's make this more precise. What are the desires the market responds to? Following the American Dream, we want a great career and material success. There are many Cinderellas and princes on Facebook and Instagram. And many lives and deaths of salesmen and saleswomen. But after centuries of romanticism and decades of (post-)hippie culture, we also want to do something for our body and soul, to improve our inner selves. Self-improvement technologies cater to this need. Our apps and podcasts are the tools for our mental and bodily workouts, our practices of self-care, and our exercises for the soul. Digital gadgets and software are romantic technologies that accompany and support our inner journeys and help us with our exercises to become a better "me."[1] Here, too, there is a comparative aspect: the technologies enable communication and comparison through social networks. We see how others are working out and working on their souls. We see their efforts and their suffering. We see how well or badly they are doing. We confess our own successes and failures, and they do the same.

That sounds almost like a humanist community. Very *gemütlich*. Positive. Supportive. It takes a very insensitive soul (say, that of a positive psychologist *qua* scientist) not to feel at least some of the sincere feelings, genuine suffering, and interpersonal warmth of that interpersonal communication, and not to detect the potentially transformative meanings that rise from the heartfelt confessions and personal dialogues spreading through social media like, well, *almost* like personal letters or good novels.

But make no mistake: these are no longer the old humanist self-improvement practices and not even the modern disciplinary games Foucault wrote about. With the introduction of AI and other digital technologies, something has fundamentally changed: the kind of self-knowledge and the kind of self that we are improving. While we are working out and meditating, we are tracked and, transformed into data, analyzed and sold. This means that our self becomes quantified. It is no longer the mysterious, dark, and complex self that is explored in novels and good old humanist psychology. It is not even the disciplined modern self: under the regime of AI and Big Data, I am not a number, as in modern prisons and concentration camps; I am *many numbers*. All my clicks, mouse movements, keyboard entries, and downloads are recorded and processed in computational ways, and these data move around the world and are analyzed, stored, sold, and used. Artificial intelligence is involved in this data process: with AI in the form of machine learning, large quantities of data about many people (Big Data) can be analyzed. Correlations are found, probabilities are calculated, predictions are made about what books I will buy, how much energy I will use, and whether there will be a crime in my neighborhood. But whatever is done with the data, there is also a feedback of data directed at me, for example, for the purpose of self-improvement. I see how much I have run and where, and I see the data of my body. I see my meditation and yoga performances, the likes and comments to my social media posts, and my personalized mental health advice.

This has consequences for the way I know myself and relate to myself. "Quantified self," as two *Wired* journalists called it in 2007, is not only a self-tracking practice; it is also a technology of the self. It creates a particular kind of knowledge of the self: quantified knowledge, a knowledge that can be put in numbers and that can *only* be put in numbers.[2] By engaging in these practices, I come to understand myself as a data-self. And today it is not the nurse, administrative assistant, or prison guard who takes and produces our data, as in the modern institutions analyzed by Foucault; instead, *I* play an important role in this self-knowledge creation: I am self-tracking, I produce my data

63

and measurements. We do it even in our sleep. We put ourselves under 24/7 surveillance in order to produce a self that consists of numbers, which show how well we perform with regard to our self-improvement goals. Through use of the technologies, I get the impression that I am my data. I perceive myself as a data-producing and data-processing machine.

Picking up Foucault's approach again, and keeping in mind that self-improvement was always linked to self-knowledge and self-examination, let's have a closer look at that knowledge and its relation to technology. Interestingly, it is a *new* kind of knowledge that could not have been generated with the help of the old humanist technologies and practices. Without the running app, I would not know how long exactly I was running and what my heart rate was at any given time and how this compares with the average. Without the mental health app, I would not know precisely how anxious or depressed I am as compared with other people (i.e., to which particular statistical category I belong). Without the online voting tool, I wouldn't know my political identity in terms of percentages (so much percentage left, so much percentage libertarian, etc.). It turns out that digital technologies do not only inform, compare, and track; they also generate knowledge of ourselves—quantitative knowledge—and this knowledge *we did not have without the technologies*. AI and data science play a key role in creating and analyzing that knowledge: they are tools and methods that need quantitative input, process quantitative information, and offer a quantitative output.

This is not done by one device but by an ecosystem of technologies, and it does not happen at one point in time but is a process. Digital technologies "necessitate" the sensors and other interfaces that turn analog information into digital quantitative information (data) and give us the results of data analysis in return. They "create" related technologies and practices that make sure the data are captured and that enable feedback. And this happens continuously. This entire technological setup and process then gives me a new kind of knowledge that was not available to me before digital technologies and AI, and that knowledge is related to new technologies (new sensors, e.g., in a mobile phone), infrastructures (internet via mobile data), and practices (for example, running with a phone or watch that tracks you, which creates a different kind of running). All of this together constitutes a new epistemic order, what Foucault called *episteme*, but then one with a very material and technological side to it. It is a self-improvement culture, if you wish, but it is for sure a technoculture and a techno-knowledge that flourishes here. The self that is constructed and improved in the wired and wireless data spaces of today's world might be partly created by us; it is certainly also made by AI and other technologies of quantification.

65

Moreover, often I am not aware that this is happening or the knowledge that is generated is not available to me at all. When the capturing or analysis is done without my knowledge or consent, I don't even know the numbers related to me, let alone what is or was done with them. For example, I may know that a particular website or app tracks me but be totally ignorant about what data are taken, what is done with the data, and how the information that is fed back to me is generated. Even if I consent, I might not know exactly what the AI algorithm does or did, how it was trained (on which data), and who made the decisions about all this. I also may not know what exactly third parties do with my data, even if I have given my consent to them. Giving consent is often a blanket that covers up a lot of things we do not know or are not supposed to know. In particular, we are not told that our data are monetized and how. We are told, instead, that we are *improving ourselves*.

Therefore, there are at least two senses in which *AI knows me better than myself.* First, it generates a new kind of knowledge, quantitative knowledge, about myself. Its operations are not neutral to how I understand myself: it shapes a very particular way of understanding myself. Second, it not only has access to information about me that I did not have before; I may also not have access to that information at all, for example when the data are captured and analyzed afterward without my awareness. If what AI does is invisible, AI knows more *and those who employ AI* know more about me than I do.

To be sure, this new kind of knowledge and this hidden data economy enables AI and its invisible employers to function as coach, therapist, and trainer: they can give training instructions (remember the imperative: Exercise! Train!) and tell us how we can improve ourselves. This sounds empowering. But this AI-driven knowledge process also gives those same agents power over us. Paradoxically, the self-improvement technologies that were meant, among other things, to empower us and hence seemed to support the realization of ancient self-control and modern Enlightenment autonomy turn into instruments for manipulation and exploitation, having us achieve the very opposite of what we wanted: loss of control and heteronomy. Through tracking, surveillance, and manipulation, others set our self-improvement goals for us and define how we can reach them. The app tells us what to do, when to do it, how to do it, and what target we need to reach. I am still busy with "self-improvement," but what counts as (knowledge of the) self and what goals need to be reached are at least jointly defined by the technology and those who made it and benefit from it. The *claim* is that the technology empowers me, but it turns out that, through the technology, I am also surprisingly dependent on other people and the things they develop and market. The ancient Stoic philosopher shivers when confronted with such a perversion of his self-improvement advice.

Note, however, that the new kind of knowledge generated by the technology is always cogenerated by humans: the users and the developers of the technology. This is true in general but also even at the technical level and the level of data science: the analysis done by AI is still informed by other kinds of knowledge. Data scientists call this "domain knowledge." For example, ideally a meditation app is built with the help of experts in meditation. In addition, AI can also help with, and *transform*, traditional methods of self-improvement such as education and various forms of psychotherapy, in which AI helps patients to construct self-knowledge.[3] Already in the 1960s the program ELIZA, one of the first chatbots, was used to simulate interaction between a psychologist and a patient. Created at MIT's Artificial Intelligence Laboratory by Joseph Weizenbaum, the program would interact with users via text (in the form of a dialogue) and give users the illusion that they were understood by the machine. It was meant as a parody of what a nondirectional psychotherapist does, but some people had the feeling that the machine understood them. In the 1980s traditional AI was applied to clinical contexts, and Sherry Turkle explored bridges between the worlds of AI and psychoanalysis.[4] Today machine learning and natural language processing are used to develop new applications in psychotherapy. For example, while not replacing the therapist, machine learning can help to identity mental illnesses.[5] Insofar as AI is involved, this also produces, or at least helps to produce, knowledge of the self that the client does not have access to without the technology. Again, AI knows you better than you know yourself. And, perhaps surprisingly, the same is true for the therapist: AI knows the client better than the therapist. Before the client talks, the AI already knows how she feels—or at least is able to produce a very specific kind of knowledge about her, a kind of knowledge that neither the client nor the therapist could have gained without the technology.

Now, if AI knows you better than yourself, it seems that ancient care of the self and humanist methods for self-improvement are obsolete altogether. In *Homo Deus*, historian Yuval Noah Harari writes that, according to "Dataism," the new emerging techno-religion which worships data, you can do without the wisdom offered by ancient religions and humanist efforts to get in touch with yourself by, for example, keeping a diary or talking with a good friend about your feelings. Algorithms know how you feel. You better listen to them. "Know yourself" remains the imperative, but for that we now have Google, Facebook, DNA sequencing, and wearable devices: "The Google and

Facebook algorithms not only know exactly how you feel, they also know a million other things about you that you hardly suspect. Consequently you should now stop listening to your feelings, and start listening to these external algorithms instead."[6]

AI thus provides an opportunity to gain new knowledge about ourselves, albeit knowledge of a very particular kind. Moreover, according to the narrative of Dataism, AI will evolve in ways we can neither control nor understand: "it follows its own path, going where no human has gone before—and where no human can follow."[7] In such a world, it is doubtful if there is still a place for the human as we know it. Humanist resistance seems futile. Our best chance seems to be human enhancement. We need an upgrade.

IMPROVEMENT IS NOT GOOD ENOUGH: ENHANCEMENT THROUGH BIOTECHNOLOGIES AND AI

Traditional methods and techniques of self-improvement in ancient and humanist times always assumed that there was a human nature to work with. Self-improvement then meant becoming the perfect human—usually: the perfect *man*. Although in his *Oration on the Dignity of the Human Being* the humanist Pico della Mirandola argued that we can shape our own life through our choices and that humans can become "a heavenly animal"[8] if we they cultivate their intellectual capacities, all these possibilities still lie within human nature. Other religious ideals of perfection also started from such a human essence. Human nature and the human condition were accepted as given. It was even highly advisable to do so, since it was assumed that they are unchangeable. In creational religious language: we didn't make ourselves. In the language of evolutionary biology: we evolved. Through evolution, we became what we are. Darwin challenged creational thinking, but not the idea that we have to work with what we are now— what we have become through evolution. Traditional self-improvement ideas take human nature as given, and work with it to educate and improve humans as they are "found," so to speak.

But this changes when new technological possibilities open up that seem to promise what is usually referred to as "human enhancement": the improvement or "enhancement" of the human mind and body itself by new *technological* means. Human nature is no longer taken as given. Humanism is replaced by *transhumanism*. The goal is to overcome the human, not just at the individual level or using traditional methods such as techniques to achieve more self-control and autonomy or humanist education with books, but by means of changing and augmenting the human itself. The human as it is found is seen as not good enough: too stupid, to ugly, too slow, to weak, too often failing to perform and to do the right thing. Time for an upgrade, time for Human 2.0. The goal of humanist self-improvement is replaced by transhumanist self-enhancement, at an individual level and at the level of the species. According to Ray Kurzweil, Nick Bostrom, Natasha Vita-More, Kevin Warwick, Hans Moravec, Ben Goertzel, John Harris, and others, it is high time to do this. Enhancement will enable us to overcome unnecessary limitations such as disease and suffering, perhaps even aging, and give us new capacities. Rather than accept and embrace the human condition, as humanists do, we should alter it.

And things are going to change anyway. In *The Singularity Is Near*, inventor and futurist Ray Kurzweil writes about the acceleration of machine intelligence, culminating in the "singularity," when humans will upload themselves and transcend the limitations of their biological bodies and brains. But also before that happens, we can enhance ourselves by using all kinds of technologies. For example, John Harris proposes using biotechnology to alter the human genome, thus replacing or enhancing Darwinian evolution.[9] And perhaps we should extend ourselves with machines. Engineering professor Kevin Warwick is famous for his work on direct interfaces between computers and the human nervous system. In this book *I, Cyborg*, Warwick tells how he did experiments on himself, putting technological implants in his body by means of surgery.

For transhumanists all this is possible, acceptable, and desirable since, according to them, we are already machines: biological machines, but machines nevertheless. Giving us an upgrade or an extension is then not a problem, at least not conceptually or morally; rather, it is required. It is a technological and scientific challenge, and it is a means of participating in a story of increasing and expanding intelligence. Moreover, it is assumed that digital technologies can render the brain and mind fully transparent. The idea is that the technology can go where no technology could go before. Using fMRI scanning in combination with computer models, neuroscientists try to read people's minds.[10]

No Socratic or humanist self-knowledge needed here; the machine will tell you what you think and who you are. It will tell you if you lie and how moral you are. It will store your identity in the form of data. Transhumanists dream of uploading the mind to a digital sphere, thus enabling people to achieve immortality. Moreover—and here I fully agree—we have always used technologies to enhance ourselves. We have always been cyborgs. Think of our humanist who reads and writes books. If he wears glasses, he is a kind of cyborg: a combination of biology and technology. But the point is a more profound one: would he be the same person, and would he even be the humanist he became, without the medium of the book and the technology of the printing press? Is and was he not already a cyborg?

But back to artificial intelligence. AI is often seen as a technology that concerns intelligence in machines. But it can also be used for human enhancement. Some believe that this can be done in the form of directly linking the human brain to a computer. Think again about Warwick's experiments: we could try to connect digital technology to our nervous system, perhaps even our brains. Scientists are already developing brain-computer interfaces. According to Kurzweil, enhancing our brains is necessary in order to prevent AI machines taking over control. He envisages a merging of mind and machines.[11] But AI can also be used as a tool to enhance human intelligence, memory, decision making, and communication without a physical brain-computer interface or biotechnological changes. Some explore the use of AI to assist moral decision making, leading to what is called "moral enhancement": Julian

Savulescu and Hannah Maslen have argued that AI could give advice on the right course of action, helping people to do the right thing based on their own values and overcoming natural psychological limitations.[12] They claim that this would enhance the agent's autonomy. In other words: Stoicism on steroids, or more precisely, modern autonomy thinking supported by AI. Kant would be shocked by what he likely would see as a denial and bypassing of human autonomy, a refusal of humanity to grow up. But transhumanists are eager to help the fallible, imperfect, and miserable humans to do what is right. Francisco Lara and Jan Deckers even give AI a "Socratic" role: the machine would "ask relevant questions and reveal potential failures in the argumentation."[13] Could AI replace philosophers, for example, by being more rational than most humans?

In addition, one could also envisage AI that helps us to change our state of consciousness, for example via audio technology or perhaps also virtual and augmented reality (VR and AR).[14] In the 1980s, the CIA investigated the "Gateway Experience" technique to alter consciousness and escape the confines of space of time. Using audio techniques developed by Bob Monroe, known for his explorations of out-of-body experiences, the researchers tried to create a state in which minds would not only have out-of-body experiences but also be able to move to the past and even into the future.[15] And in an article in *Frontiers in Psychiatry*, Giuseppe Riva and colleagues suggest that VR and AR could not only be used for creating experiences of different external environments (e.g., for the purpose of entertainment or training), but also for transforming our *inner* experience by altering our bodily self-consciousness. For example, VR could be used for so-called "full body swapping" in which someone's body is substituted by a virtual body that is then experienced as one's own. According to the authors, this would mean that, as in the movie *Being John Malkovich*, we can experience the perspective of someone else.[16] Perhaps AI could assist these consciousness-alteration techniques. For example, AI can produce binaural audio, which then can stimulate the brain in various ways in order to help the mind to reach a different level of consciousness.

Note that there are of course also other ways of changing consciousness that aim for fast-track spirituality: drugs. For example, so-called *entheogens* are psychoactive substances that induce alterations in mood and cognition in ways that are meant to promote spiritual development. Traditionally they are used in for example shamanic rituals and in the indigenous cultures of the Americas (for example, use of ayahuasca), and in the 1960s they used to be called psychedelic drugs, but also today various new and old substances are used for this purpose, for example by new religious movements in the United States and Brazil. AI joins this range of conscious-altering technologies of the self and what one may call *spiritual technologies* or technologies for the soul.

In sum, the idea is that AI would help us to make up our mind and potentially change our mind and consciousness. In this way, AI could thus become a powerful tool for self-improvement, now understood as self-*enhancement*: improvement beyond "normal" human capabilities by technological means.

This transhumanist and high-tech approach to self-improvement, self-enhancement, significantly differs from the traditional ways of improving yourself. Consider again the idea of moral enhancement. People who use Socratic methods and Stoic techniques, or people who embrace modern autonomy and even existentialist choice, do not aim to improve themselves beyond what humans can achieve. Instead, they try to become fully human and, in some cases, fully themselves. As Lara and Deckers acknowledge, Socrates helped people recollect ideas that were already there. Stoics and, say, Kantian reasoners try to improve their morality in order to become more fully human, defined then in a particular way: humans are rational beings and have to realize that human nature. Going *beyond* the human and beyond human possibilities is not on the agenda. Moreover, the idea in these methods is that you achieve control and do the right thing by your own efforts. The Stoic tries to control her own desires. The Kantian tries to be moral for its own sake, not because it makes her feel better. The purpose is to be moral against natural inclinations, and this is to be done by training one's own mind. All this requires considerable mental effort, and the very idea of self-improvement is linked to being able to do this yourself. Using a machine to help overcome one's natural inclination seems like using a shortcut that does not really improve the self—at least not according to such traditional views. It is a way of outsourcing the hard self-improvement work to the machine. It is crossing out the "self" in "self-improvement." The same can be said in response to proposals for altering one's state of consciousness: the new technologies seem to promise fast-track enlightenment, but—if what they promise is possible at all—it remains doubtful if we really improve, spiritually, mentally, or otherwise.

There are also (more) ethical and political problems with using AI for these purposes of decision support and self-enhancement. For example, there is the danger of paternalism: What if the machine serves the values and interests of other people, rather than your own? As is well-known by now, AI can be biased or perpetuate existing and historical bias. It may well help you to make a decision, but that decision could be biased due to the data used by the AI and due to the algorithm. The technology is not politically neutral. For example, an AI algorithm trained on data of previous hires in a company may suggest that extrovert white male candidates are the best, not because they are better, but just because they happen to have been hired previously. And we can imagine that a future advanced AI trained on data from an individualist society may see it as moral improvement that everyone only cares about themselves, even if that harms others. It is also far from clear and uncontroversial that control of your desires is always a good thing. Often proposals for such "moral machines" come with a range of assumptions about morality; they may even promote a particular way of thinking about morality, to the exclusion of other normative approaches. For example, they may promote the idea that being moral and doing the right thing is only or mainly about smart reasoning and following reason. They may also encourage a particular version of the good life, for example, a Stoic one. Whether or not those particular views and ways of life are valuable, the point is that relying on AI and other technologies does not relieve us of the task and burden of examining ourselves and our society and finding out what the good life is. Once we have technologies that claim to know what the right thing to do is and what is good for us, we might too easily abandon that quest and fully trust the technology. In that sense, we don't need trustworthy AI. We need philosophers: those who desire wisdom, not just clever reasoning or statistical and quantitative forms of knowledge. Technology may well be able to help in various spheres of life, but it cannot be a substitute for the hard work of gaining self-knowledge and becoming wiser.

The good news is that others can help us with this. Put in stronger terms: self-improvement is only possible with the help of others. This takes us to the next chapters. What is the solution to the present self-improvement crisis?

6

The Solution (Part I)

Relational Self and Social Change

This book is not against improving yourself; that's been a good idea since ancient times. What's problematic is the specific shape it has taken today, which is the result of an entire history, culture, society, economy, and technology connected to it. The previous chapters have shown how ideas about self-knowledge and self-improvement have been mixed with and further developed by a number of other ideas and societal developments, which eventually has culminated in self-improvement practices and environments that are ethically problematic, politically harmful, and physically and mentally unhealthy. Therefore, the solution to this collective obsession and self-improvement crisis is not, and cannot be, to abandon self-improvement altogether. It might well be worth preserving it, but not in its present form; we need to find a better way of improving ourselves and our society.

Similarly, this book is not an argument against technology. It's not against AI or against social media and the

internet. The previous chapters made it clear that the problem is not just about technology. What renders self-
improvement problematic and what makes us sick is the
combination with the different factors mentioned. Technology plays an important role in creating both the opportunities and the problems, for sure, but it is not the only
problem, and it is hardly *ever* a problem on its own. That's
because technology is human through and through: it's
intrinsically entangled with people, societies, and cultures.
Humans develop it. Humans use it. And humans bear the
consequences. If there are dangers in AI at all, it's because
we are dangerous: because we, by developing and using
these technologies and by other means, made this a dangerous place to live in.

If we want to find a solution to the self-improvement
crisis, therefore, we need to look at the whole picture,
learn lessons from the multifaceted analysis offered in
the previous chapters, and identify some deeper, underly-
ing problems. Let's start with questioning the idea that
we need to work on the self and even the "self" in
"self-improvement."

WORKING ON THE SELF VERSUS
SELF-DEVELOPMENT AND GROWTH
AS NARRATIVE SELVES

The idea that self-improvement and self-development
are mainly or even exclusively a matter of self-knowledge,
work, and training is not obvious. It assumes that we can
fully know ourselves, and that what we are and become is

entirely under our control and is exclusively a matter of setting our own goals. That the self is transparent to us and a product of self-work and that we can design the self according to a self-made concept. But is this so?

First, as Freud and later postmodern thinkers such as Jacques Lacan have argued, the self is not totally transparent to itself. Freud thought that there is the unconscious: a part of the mind that influences but that we are not aware of. If this is true, then we cannot fully know ourselves. We are always to some extent a mystery to ourselves. There is a stranger within us, an other. What we thought was the self is also always a little bit alien, uncanny, something that is familiar to us but at the same time strange.[1] The self is not a bright living room with transparent windows; it is more like the dark cellar underneath. We are afraid of the monster, but the monster is in us. And external things such as language, culture, and technology shape us, make us into what we are. In Lacan, the modern intimate self is replaced by a postmodern *extimate* one.[2] The interior starts to feel exterior. The living room becomes invaded and stirred by the city. What we are "inside" is shaped by the "outside." This means that both the Enlightenment *and* the ancient ideals of self-improvement are mistaken when they assume that it is possible to fully know and autonomously shape ourselves. We cannot give the law to ourselves when the law (the others, the language, the rules, etc.) is already in us. The same is true, *a fortiori*, for self-enhancement visions: when the self is not a fixed essence that can be made transparent, it is impossible to upgrade or upload it. What we don't know cannot be controlled, let alone enhanced.

Second, in this picture of the self in self-improvement there should not only be more room for what is not under our control and what is not intended; too much effort at control and too much goal-directedness may also be *counterproductive* for improving our selves and create its own problems.

A helpful comparison is happiness. Frantically searching for happiness or trying to become happy is seldom seen as something that actually makes one happy. If we are too obsessed with the goal, the goal may not be reached at all. Our search for happiness is then in the way of realizing it. Moreover, contrary to what ancient Stoic wisdom suggests, human happiness is always partly dependent on others and on what happens outside our control. While it's true that we should not become the slave of others' opinions, as Rousseau warned, it is simply impossible to entirely find happiness within oneself. It also depends on others and it depends on some luck. The same seems true for self-improvement. Whether we like it or not, we are social beings and what we are (our self) is to a significant extent shaped by those we are related to. We can improve and develop ourselves and see this as our own task and effort. But if we actually improve and develop in the process, that's not just a result of our work; it is also a by-product of whatever it is we do, what others do and say, and whatever happens around us—things that are not under our control, or at least not fully. People and things that challenge and help us. Others *can* be a barrier to self-improvement, for sure, but more often than not, they also help us to improve ourselves. Those around us also make us into the person we are and we grow in relation to them and partly because of them.

Think of a good novel, or any good story for that matter: the main character only emerges in the course of the story, that is, it grows organically in the course of its interactions with others; what it "is" is defined by those others and those interactions.[3] The same is true for the self and human life, which also have a narrative structure. What I am is not designed, and I cannot relate to it as if it is an artifact or product that is ready and transparent on beforehand; it emerges only in the course of my life as I interact with others and respond to events. I become. The self is not a thing but a story.

In psychology and philosophy this is called "narrative identity." The French philosopher Paul Ricoeur has developed an account of narrativity in which the self emerges through narrative: through our story and through the ways we experience, interpret, and imagine.[4] Only through and after the story do meaning and self develop. Similarly, Charles Taylor has argued that to get a sense of who we are, we have to have an idea of "how we have become, and of where we are going."[5] Making sense of ourselves and our lives in a narrative way relates past, present, and future. We do not only want to give meaning to particular events but to our self and our lives as a whole. What and who I am is thus a matter of interpretation and self-interpretation, and that's mediated by narrativity. The self is an evolving story.

If that's true, then the modern conception of the self and therefore also the modern conception of self-improvement need revision. To be sure, the existentialists are right that we are not an essence. We can create new stories and incorporate new stories into our own. This is a kind of freedom to shape the self. But neither does it follow that we are completely free to create that self. We cannot fully give the story to ourselves; we cannot always be character and author at the same time. And a narrative is never just about the actions of a character. There are also a lot of things that happen outside the control of the character. More generally, my sense-making is always mediated by the narratives and meanings that are already present in my culture. This includes ideas of what is important. Taylor calls these "horizons of significance": what I am is not only self-created but also involves things that are not decided, things that are given.[6] And according to Alasdair MacIntyre, individual life stories are "embedded in social traditions."[7] As a modern individual, I may want to be authentic and I may want control of my life and of what I am. Think again about Berlin's definition of positive freedom or autonomy. Autonomy is a good thing, it's a value. We desire to create and improve ourselves. And we should try to be authentic, in the sense that what we are is not *merely* what others say we are or should be. We rightly want to be the author of our lives. But it is important to recognize that this can be only a coauthorship or limited authorship: I will never get full control, full autonomy, and full freedom with regard to myself and my story. Improving the self, then, is not a matter of design, as the existentialists thought (and transhumanists want to realize via technology). It is a process and a story that I influence but over which I have no full control.

Moreover, in line with Freud and Lacan, and in contrast to what the AI-driven quantitative and empirical-psychological approaches to the self suggest, Ricoeur also argues that the self is not completely transparent. Our access to ourselves is mediated by language. We have to interpret ourselves. Sometimes we only understand ourselves in hindsight, after a part of our life story is already lived. This means again that if we are the author of ourselves at all, we are not a fully autonomous author who is completely in control. Even if I may strive for self-control and autonomy, like the Stoics and the modern philosophers, I have to accept this limitation. But, luckily, this is not only a limitation. I can see others and events outside my control as a limitation or a problem, but also as something positive and what makes the self possible in the first place. Others make me into what I am. And the narratives, horizons, and traditions that form the background of my self-making also *enable* me to make sense of my own life.

If that's right, then self-improvement is not just a matter of creation and self-creation. To highlight these aspects that have to do with lack of full control, emergence, and social relations, we can use the metaphors of development and growth. Like stories, these are better metaphors for self-improvement than work. Living beings can grow and flourish only in and through their interconnectedness with other beings and with their environment. Their dependence renders them vulnerable, but it also is a way—in fact the only way—for them to live and grow. Similarly, improving ourselves cannot just be done by turning inward and by isolating our mind from the rest of the world. We need others in order to get to know ourselves and to improve and grow ourselves. Furthermore, we also help others to achieve self-knowledge and growth. Becoming better persons—morally and in other ways—requires an ecosystem that supports us and that we in turn *give* to. In culture as in biology, the absence of mutual dependency, communication, and exchange means nothing less than death. When we use ancient techniques from West and East to improve ourselves, we should make sure that these techniques are not only aimed at preparing ourselves for death. In the first place, we should prepare for life, and indeed live. Hurried and excited as we are to improve ourselves, we might forget to live our lives and fail to grow in response to what happens to us. And in our efforts to render ourselves less vulnerable to others, we might well build up walls that also prevent the very exchanges that enable us to grow. Self-improvement is a matter of growth and development within a social, cultural, and indeed natural environment.

Another way of framing this is to say that our self is *relational*. It can exist and improve only in relation to others and the wider environment. The relationality of the self is well recognized in some Western theory of self—for example, in feminist perspectives on the self and ethics of care[8] and in deep ecology—and especially in non-Western worldviews. For example, in Confucianism, the self is fundamentally social: it is defined in terms of its social relations and roles. Self-improvement then means a better, harmonious integration into the social whole through fulfilling social obligations and developing virtues such as compassion and trustworthiness. Social harmony, not individual well-being, is the guiding principle and most cherished ideal of Confucian culture.[9] Ubuntu philosophical traditions also characterize the self in a fundamentally relational way. The Venda phrase *"muthu ndi muthu nga vhathu"* means that a person is a person through others. The Kenyan theologian John Mbiti replaced the Cartesian *cogito ergo sum* with: "I am because we are, and since we are, therefore I am."[10] Individuals are seen as deeply social: they are understood as part of the group and the community, both the living and the dead. While these perspectives on the self and related notions such as personhood cannot, and perhaps should not, be simply adopted in a Western context (they may be reduced to yet another product sold by the self-help industry or may be appropriated in a colonial way), they might provide inspiration for thinking beyond individualist approaches to self and self-improvement, and in ways that are more attentive to the diversity of philosophical traditions. To see the self as relational frames dependency on others and on the ecosystem not as a problem but as a chance for self-improvement.

Narcissistic attitudes to self-improvement miss this point about relationality and in the end lead to the creation of a dead, nonliving self: a thing, an idea, an essence that is isolated from others and the rest of the world and that no longer changes. The danger of suicide that matters for most of us in modern times is not physical death of the body but the risk of what we could call *the narcissistic suicide of the self*: a form of self-destruction that happens when we start understanding ourselves in a nonrelational way and thereby do harm to others and to ourselves. This was what happened to Narcissus: a suicide, but without his being aware of what he was doing to himself. The kind of "self-improvement" that involves such a suicide thus reaches the opposite goal of what it aimed for: the corruption and eventually the death of the self, which cannot grow and live without relations.

Moreover, the "self" in "self-improvement" is not only nontransparent and relational but perhaps it does not even exist. As we have seen earlier, Buddhism warns us for seeing the self as a thing, and it goes as far as saying that there is no permanent and fixed self. There is no separate self, if that means that there would be an entity that exist by itself. According to this doctrine in Buddhism, the self is thus radically relational—to the extent that it can be said to be illusionary. If this is true, there is no self to improve and our focus on the self as the center of the world is not only mistaken but also dangerous: self-centeredness can lead to selfishness, competition, and suffering. Then it is better that in self-improvement practices we *don't* focus on the self at all, but rather orient ourselves to others.

DIFFERENT SELVES AND BEYOND THE SELF: WHAT ABOUT (IMPROVING OUR RELATION TO) OTHERS AND THE ENVIRONMENT?

To develop such a direction and find out what it means for thinking about self-improvement and AI, let me first further explain how these ideas lead us to question the modern self that has emerged in the history of (Western) ideas and societies, the modern self that underlies our contemporary self-improvement culture.

First, since the Enlightenment there have been two modern conceptions of the self that dominate our culture, and the tension between them still fuels the debates about the ethics and politics of AI. One is the individual and independent, *autonomous* self: the self that is not ruled by an authority outside itself but gives the law to itself. Often the philosopher Immanuel Kant is seen as having articulated such the idea of such a self. But there is a connection to Rousseau's ideas about self-rule, which inspired Kant, and there is a line that goes back to the ancient Greek philosophers, who thought that you can only rule others if you first can rule yourself. Berlin's description of positive liberty draws on this: we want to be master of ourselves and our lives. Sometimes philosophers also express this in terms of free will (see also my reference to Dostoyevsky in chapter 3), although the relationship between autonomy and free will is more complex.

89

The other modern conception of the self is the self that is under surveillance and manipulated by means of social engineering. It is the *manipulated* self, the self that is entirely shaped and determined by external influences and technologies. Often this is simply done to make profit or to maintain political power. But sometimes it is well intended. For example, one idea is to use the sciences, for example social sciences and statistics, to improve society and its citizens. Here the nineteenth-century French philosopher Auguste Comte, another founding figure in sociology, is worth mentioning: he argued for a scientific approach to human behavior, which helps to understand society but also helps to optimize social control and construct a better society: social engineering. He proposed a rationalization of government, based on positive scientific knowledge. In the early twentieth century, statistics and probability theory were already used in the social sciences. And Foucault's analysis of the history of disciplinary practices comes to mind again: practices that also relied on data and statistics, albeit without using AI. The modern sciences have always helped to tame and control people, in the name of humanism and in the name of Enlightenment.

Both conceptions of the self are in tension, if not straightforward opposition. Contrary to the philosophical ideal of autonomy, the manipulated self under surveillance is a heteronomous self, one that does not self-rule and self-control but is dependent on, and controlled by, others. And the manipulated self is not treated as having capacities for rational control, authorship, or free will; instead, it is seen as a behavioristic machine that can and must be controlled. Treating people in this way is thus an insult to the ideal of the modern autonomous self.

Today we find these ideas and this tension again in discussions about artificial intelligence. Opponents of AI defend the supposedly autonomous self against threats from AI, which is used to quantify, manipulate, and engineer the self and society. In the 1990s, Gilles Deleuze used the term "societies of control."[11] After the disciplinary settings described by Foucault, there are more fluid modulations. Instead of the modern individuals, we find "dividuals" that are distributed across databases and computer files. Computers are the machines that belong to the control society.[12] They enable tracking and control. Today, AI technology intensifies such forms of control. We are no longer modern individuals but postmodern dividuals, analyzed and controlled by AI and other digital technologies. This raises again the specter of totalitarianism. However, both Foucault and Deleuze show that politics is not just a matter of top-down power exercised by governments, but that power is everywhere and (I add) is entangled with technologies. Or to put it in other words: Foucault and Deleuze show us that the (early) modern Leviathan monster, the symbol of centralized top-down government, is no more; its ashes are dispersed in the seas of data and its spirit rattles on in the almost silent and invisible work of AI algorithms, which are used to manipulate, monitor, and control us.

Interestingly, however, both the philosophers defending individual autonomy and the social engineers appeal to, and stand in the tradition of, the Enlightenment. Embracing these radical versions of Enlightenment, both sides reject traditional forms of power and replace it by self-rule and scientific control. They reject a self that is determined by traditional society and replace that self with one that is either entirely autonomous or entirely controlled—top-down and otherwise.

Yet, in light of what I said about the relational, narrative, and growing self, but also taking into account lessons from contemporary philosophy of technology, both conceptions of the self are deeply problematic. Humanists and proponents of Rousseauvian and Kantian Enlightenment are right that our selves cannot and should not be reduced to data and that control by others is undesirable and wrong. But neither are our selves autonomous. They are shaped by others, but also by the technologies and technological environments they grow in. Our selves are not only socially but also technologically relational. This has been so since the beginning of *Homo sapiens*, who was always already a social being and a *Homo technologicus* in the sense of a user of tools. We have always been closely related to technology. We have always been cyborgs. And we have always used technologies for self-improvement; this *in itself* is not a problem but simply an aspect of human existence and human becoming.

With AI, this entanglement of humans and machines takes on new forms. If we want to improve ourselves, we had better acknowledge that it is impossible to create a self that is isolated from others or from technology. While we should reject the totally heteronomous self that is controlled and *dividuated*, a fully autonomous self would not be an improvement; it would be no longer human at all. Therefore, an appeal to autonomy cannot and should not be used to reject AI on the grounds that it is a technology and that therefore it threatens the self by definition. The self is already both social and technological, and the only kind of autonomy worth wanting is one that recognizes that relational dependence, which is not just limiting but also enabling.

However, recognizing this existential dependence on technologies does not necessarily imply that we *are* technologies. The contemporary self-improvement concept is fueled by the relatively recent, rather extraordinary idea that we are an artifact: the self is a work of art and technology that can be built from scratch. Existentialism has developed this idea to its full radicality, and today it reappears in the transhumanist ideal of the upgraded, transhuman self: we are what we make of ourselves. But this is mistaken. Of course we have *some* freedom to steer our life and to shape ourselves—although that depends on the community and society we live in. But we are not created, not even by ourselves. We are born. We grow and develop. And we are not permanent. We will die. Technology cannot change this. It is true that, as the existentialists argued, we exist and we do not have an essence. But if we are not a thing, as Sartre stressed, then that also means that we are not an artifact. The self is not a tool, and we are not its engineers or designers.

There is some room for change and improvement. It is true that we can, and perhaps should, change the human to some extent: consider for example how modern medicine has already increased the life span of people and how genetic engineering might eradicate some genetic diseases. But we are, and always have been, developing in interaction with our environment, with the body that we are born with and that changes, and with the people and the society and culture in which we find ourselves. We are only partly made. We can only partly choose. We are not completely free with regard to what we are. We can change only to some extent. There is a cultural horizon. and there are biological limitations and barriers raised by the natural environments we live in. None of these limits are fixed; borders can be crossed and perhaps should be crossed in some cases. Perhaps border-crossing is itself part of the horizon of modern and Western cultures. Technology pushes the limits, crosses borders—including the borders of the earth and even the borders of the self, entering what was known as the "intimate" and "inner" sphere. Technology is a Promethean protest, an attempt to help ourselves rather than submitting to what the gods want from us. But there are limits to self-improvement if that means self-fabrication. However much we may regret it, we are not a designed product or a work of art. Much of what we call "self" is given. Just as the influential philosopher, anthropologist, and sociologist Bruno Latour argued that our societies have never been modern, one could say that we have never been modern selves.[13] We make choices and act. But we have always been shaped by everything and everyone on which we depend: social and cultural environments, technological environments, natural environments, and so on. We are relational and environmental beings through and through.

94

Therefore, if we want to improve ourselves, we had better start by accepting ourselves, acknowledging the limits to self-knowledge, opening ourselves to others, and responding to our environment in ways that make us grow. If we must love ourselves, then we should develop the kind of self-love that Rousseau recommended: a self-love that does not always compare. A self-love that also accepts. And such self-love includes sparing ourselves the obsessive kind of self-improvement work, which often goes at the expense of ourselves and others, and thereby destroys what it wanted to improve. If we wish to improve ourselves, we must enable growth instead of relying on work only. In order to grow, we need others and we need our environment: to receive and to give. We have already received. We have a story and a history. We better accept that we are not a blank slate, a piece of raw material, or a stem cell that can become everything: we have our narrative identity, personality, tradition, bodily and genetic limitations. We can change and improve ourselves, but we do not fully know ourselves, lack full control over ourselves, and cannot become everything. Absolute autonomy and self-making are impossible. We better embrace ourselves and our limitations, even if these limitations are not fixed. And the limitations are at the same time enabling conditions. We are vulnerable, dependent, and developing in interaction with all that we call not-self or other. Self and not-self are bound together in a necessary and perhaps tragic embrace.

Indeed, this relationality and dependence is not just positive, let alone always enjoyable, and acceptance of self does not mean passivity. We must respond and gain some control, push back, and take action. As persons, we must develop agency with the help of others and against others. As a species, we use the natural environment in order to survive, and this is not always a romantic picknick or a happy-ending story since there are many risks that we try to mitigate with the help of technology. Self-acceptance does not mean that we should not use modern science and technology to deal with risks and problems. AI can play a role in that. It is one of the new tools we have to help us deal with our vulnerability.[14]

Moreover, we find ourselves in a particular social environment, a society, and this society supports us and partly makes us into what we are but also presents its own dangers and puts up barriers. Keeping in mind Rousseau's lesson in *Emile*, we better do not let ourselves be tyrannized by others (and by ourselves) by always comparing ourselves to others. Sometimes it helps to say "F*ck it all," as Karen Karbo puts it.[15] We should resist societal pressures to fix ourselves. We should not listen to what marketeers, social media influencers, and advertisers tell us, and we better not care too much about what others think of us. Karbo is especially concerned with how women's insecurities are exploited, especially insecurities about how they look. But with Rousseau we can recommend this kind of emancipation to all: people find themselves in highly competitive social environments and struggle with that, sometimes in the same way, sometimes in different ways. It is wise to not make one's happiness and improvement totally dependent on others. To say it using Karbo's idiomatic repertoire: society often sucks. Some stoicism seems healthy in this respect. Without it, self-improvement and even the improvement of others seems impossible.

In general, we can find inspiration in ancient wisdom traditions for self-improvement, and change our attitude. This can be ancient ideas from non-Western cultures (Buddhism and Confucianism, for example), but also Western ancient philosophical traditions such as Stoicism or Epicureanism. The ancient quest for self-knowledge and for finding the good life is still relevant today. We are not condemned to be free, as Sartre said—at least if this suggests that we are totally free to make ourselves into whatever we want. But as human beings we are certainly condemned to try to find ourselves and live a good life. Existentialism and modern philosophical anthropology were right that, in contrast to animals, we are not fixed. As Nietzsche put it in *Beyond Good and Evil*: we are *das noch nicht festgestellte Tier*, the animal whose type has not been determined, that has not been fixed. We have an openness in this sense: the human has no fixed borders. Posthumanism is right about that. My way of putting this is that we always define ourselves in relation to others; we are relational beings. Humans use other humans and nonhumans to define themselves. Moreover, we are also self-conscious beings, and this opens up room for, and even necessitates, self-shaping and self-improvement, albeit much less room than moderns and existentialists have assumed. At most, we can *influence* our self-development. In spite of an entire culture that suggests otherwise, we neither make nor remake ourselves. Philosophy and technologies such as AI can help with shaping this influencing. But if we are too obsessed with self-improvement, we might miss the aim and become a self that is not worth striving for.

Yet these recommendations might sound too much like self-help advice and invoke the current self-improvement culture all over again. They can easily be written up as self-help one-liners and books that can be sold to masses of people hungry and desperate for self-improvement in a world that mercilessly nurtures that desire. Moreover, and more fundamentally, change of self is so difficult because of the technological, social, and economic environments and practices that are already in place, environments in which we find ourselves. Paradoxically and given the relational nature of the self, if we want to change ourselves, we need also and simultaneously to change the technological, social, and economic environment. Karbo's individualist f*ck-it-all attitude or modern individualist interpretations of ancient wisdom lessons are not enough, since a focus on the individual is not enough. We cannot really change ourselves if we don't change the society we live in. From Rousseau we can learn that we can become ourselves and grow morally only in the right kind of political order. If we must use such language at all, the way forward is not "f*ck you, I turn away from you and your miserable society," but rather, "hey, why don't we change the system if the system is f*cked up?"

DIFFERENT SOCIETIES: THERE IS NO SELF-IMPROVEMENT WITHOUT SOCIAL CHANGE

Let me unpack this. From the previous discussion it is clear that we should avoid individualist (and *dividualist*) solutions and go in a more relational direction. But what does that mean? One way to interpret this is that we should take another attitude: be less self-centered and reevaluate our relation to others. This was my advice in the previous section, and it's in line with at least one recent, refreshing idea in the discussion about self-improvement. In his book *Stand Firm: Resisting the Self-Improvement Craze*, the Danish psychologist Svend Brinkmann criticizes the seemingly accelerating pace of life and the demand to keep up, adapt, and improve ourselves. Inspired by Stoic philosophy but stressing other-directedness, he recommends that we forget about self-help and instead accept ourselves and focus on the aim of coexisting peacefully with others. Stop the navel-gazing. This seems good advice: let's turn to others, to nature, without comparing all the time. Paradoxically, the idea here is not to turn inward but *outward* in order to know yourself. A healthy inversion of the ancient Stoic imperative, or at least an inversion of the "turn inward" interpretation that it has been given in the history of ideas. And I add: accept that neither full self-knowledge (the mind remains a mystery) nor full self-control (the mind as construction site) is possible. Probably it is not even desirable. With Nietzsche, one could say: don't focus so much on self-taming, don't forget to live, affirm life!

But this anti–self-help guide is still about self, about psychology, about our individual attitudes and behavior. In order to really go beyond the focus on self and individuals, a truly social and political approach is needed in addition to views of the self borrowed from ancient wisdom, non-Western perspectives, and contemporary psychology. In order to avoid falling into the trap of yet another self-help exercise, another advice to improve yourself, it is important to realize that getting out of the self-improvement crisis also requires collective action and social change. As we have seen in chapters 4 and 5, the problem is not just about individuals, but is also situated at the societal and socioeconomic level. Narcissism is a societal and cultural problem. And inspired by Marx and his contemporary interpreters, I suggested that true self-improvement is possible only if we end exploitative socioeconomic relations. We need to get away from the idea that it's completely your own responsibility to improve yourself. Stoicism, modern Protestant culture, and, more generally, a focus on the self and on self-improvement risks putting all the burden of change on individuals. Maintaining that direction is therefore not only a potential source of wisdom but also, ironically, one of the causes of the present self-improvement crisis. Next to developing a self that is more directed to others and to nature, we also need to change the system. Instead of stoicism for slaves, we need to create a society for free people who can work on their self-realization and self-improvement in a way that truly empowers and improves them, also politically.

This *political* way of thinking about the self, which in Western philosophy can already be found to some extent in Rousseau, Marx, Dewey, and MacIntyre (among others), and which has ancient roots in Aristotle's thinking, does not start from individuals, as most modern ethics and political philosophy does, but begins from acknowledging what Aristotle called in his *Politics* the political nature of human beings. Aristotle argued that we are by nature *political animals*. By this he didn't mean that we all want to go into politics (if that means become professional "politicians" in its contemporary sense), but rather that we are what we would now call *social* beings and citizens. Our happiness and flourishing require that we partner up with others and live in communities. According to Aristotle, the city (*polis*) was particularly suitable for this. By talking to one another, we can figure out how to live together. Philosophers such as Rousseau, MacIntyre, and in a sense also Marx and Dewey followed Aristotle's political view of the self. For these thinkers, human sociability is crucial. If we want or need to talk about a self at all, then we should understand that this self can develop only in a social and political environment.

Yet acknowledging this social nature of self-development does not necessarily mean that we accept the social environment as it is. Quite to the contrary, the aforementioned modern thinkers are known for having argued for social change. Rousseau was against modern society, Marx against capitalist society, Dewey against a society that is not sufficiently democratic, communicative, and science-friendly (which sounds like a familiar topic in the post-Trump era), and MacIntyre against a society that denies the value of community. Today we can learn from these thinkers when dealing with the current self-improvement crisis. If we really want to move beyond the obsession with self-improvement, we also need to reject the society that makes us into such beings, that shapes ourselves in such ways. If we don't want to be rats in the rat race, we have to do something about the rat race, and not just talk about how rats can help themselves, making small improvements to their terrible lives. If what is going wrong here is also a societal issue, let's change that society for the better. Social change is a way to avoid organized narcissism. Improving society can help us to improve ourselves in ways that are more healthy and less destructive.

Self-improvement is then a welcome by-product of improving society. If Aristotle and his intellectual heirs are right, then social change, rather than neohippie self-gazing or obsessive and narcissistic hipster self-improvement, really empowers us and makes us better people. If we were no longer part of an exploitative and competitive socioeconomic environment, and if we lived in an open and democratic political community where we really could talk together about how to shape our common future, then improving ourselves would no longer be the uphill struggle it is now: we would be able to improve ourselves as we would partly *be* improved by living in such environments. According to such a social and political approach to self-improvement, the burden of improvement is then no longer on the shoulders of the individual, crushed by modern-Protestant individualist morality that puts all the responsibility on the individual, atomistic self. Improvement is then a common goal, something we need to achieve together—and can do so only together.

Here is again some good news: contrary to what the reader might have concluded from the previous chapters, people of the new generations are not *all* obsessive self-improvers, and even if they are, they are not only busy with themselves. Today, many young people not only work on themselves; they are also interested in living differently from previous generations and yearn for a different kind of social system. Many feel that time for change has come and that things are already changing. Many millennials and zoomers care about the world and the planet, and they actually take action and protest. Think about the Occupy movement, think about movements that call attention to the climate crisis, think about the many people who change their diets for ethical and environmental reasons: there is a sense of crisis, but also a sense of the need for change at both the individual and the societal level. Teenagers and students want a different world and feel that they deserve a better world, and they are right.

However, as the history of the twentieth century shows, there are also dangers connected with attempts to create a better society as a project of *radical* social change. There is the danger of utopianism and totalitarianism. Just as it is mistaken to think that people's selves are blank slates that can and should then be entirely created, made, and fabricated, societies are also not entirely "makeable"—and if so, then only at a great human and environmental cost. Just like selves, human social worlds are not entirely transparent. Societies are human-created (and hence can and must be changed), but not in the same way as technological objects. They have their own development, and we cannot fully understand what is going on. Nor should we want to change everything. I can replace my phone, but I cannot replace an entire society. Attempts to do so come at a great cost. Extreme forms of capitalism and socialism have built new worlds but also killed and destroyed a lot: people, economies, environments. And once part of the social fabric is gone, it cannot easily be restored, because it is not like a machine that can be replaced, repaired, or upgraded. As with regard to the self, one should acknowledge that in the present society and culture there are some givens and that there may be value in some these givens. Society is not, and should not be, just what it makes of itself. It is not entirely an artifact. It evolves and has its own dynamics. It has a history. Social change can be good but, in some forms, it can also destroy a social ecosystem and communities that are already there and that function or even flourish. Therefore, it is not recommended to simply replace the project of self-engineering by the project of social engineering. Strange as it may sound in the light of the contemporary obsession with self-improvement, the belief that technology will fix it all, and the twentieth-century history of political bulldozing and deleting, there are, and there should be, limits to what we can do and should do to ourselves and to society in the name of change and improvement.

Yet it is not easy to avoid all forms of social engineering, given the societies we have built. Once you have forms of mass social organization such as nation-states and capitalist power structures in place, *some* forms of social

engineering—by means of statistics and AI, for example—
seem unavoidable. Organizing masses requires Big Data
and intelligence. Coordination at higher levels may well
require the use of AI. Once you create a "society" of individuals and *dividuals*, the damage is already done, and
change becomes harder. With today's new technological
possibilities, the idea of an AI Leviathan that ensures social
coordination becomes tempting: Why not use AI to steer
and control the social order in a desirable direction? For
example, could it be a way to deal with climate change?
Should AI take over because humans are too stupid, as the
famous Gaia theorist and scientist James Lovelock has
argued in his book *Novacene: The Coming Age of Hyperintel-
ligence*? And can this be done without compromising on
freedom?[16]

If we want to avoid such political and technological
Leviathan scenarios, as I think we should, we must try to
imagine different forms of social organization that do not
necessitate these forms of control and are not supported
by it. Perhaps we still need some political structures that
can deal with larger-scale and even global problems, but it
is worth considering alternative ways of living together
that avoid the current deadlock of (post)modern society
and control technologies. This is not only a matter of imagining distant futures. There are already attempts to set up
alternative social arrangements. There are and have been
experiments. Some people have experience with this. In
the 1970s and 1980s, but also today, with free towns, hippie
communes, eco-communities, cooperatives, monasteries,
"intentional communities," and so on.[17] Acknowledging
and studying both traditional and new, alternative ways in

which people build and maintain networks and communities bottom-up, often in spite of and against modern and postmodern forms of control, can be a step in the right direction. We need a political philosophy that is less obsessed with problems of governing nations and more with finding alternative forms of governance. After more than a century has passed, we need to finally get out of the long nineteenth century, with its toxic nationalism. We need a philosophy of the self that is linked to thinking about social change, and that needs to be a non-nationalist kind of thinking.

Another problem is that much social and political theory (including theory of social change) has neglected the role of technology and the material in its accounts of sociality and the political. Even Marx, who of course acknowledged the importance of technology as a means of production and therefore gave it a role in this account of capitalism, did not sufficiently theorize the many other ways in which technology shapes society and selves. Moreover, if technology was included in social theories, it was often seen as threatening and understood in deterministic ways. Most twentieth-century accounts of modern society have been highly pessimistic about technology. A good example here is Jacques Ellul's *The Technological Society*, which claims that *technique* and the focus on efficiency dominate society and overthrow humanity. Martin Heidegger's work on technology is also often interpreted in this way.[18] Modern technology is seen as presenting a danger. Yet in line with contemporary philosophy of technology, we can also take a different view of technology, one that is critical but at the same time gives a positive, constructive role to technology in changing ourselves and our societies,[19] one that does not exclude the possibilities that new technologies could change us in a positive way. There is also much more to say about how technology and culture are entangled. In the next chapter, I explore how technology could be part of the solution.

7

The Solution (Part II)

Technologies That Tell Different
Stories About Us

In chapter 5, I pointed to some problematic aspects of AI when it comes to self-improvement, and throughout this book I have shown how technology is an essential part of the current self-improvement culture and its history, contributing to all its ills. But could AI or other technologies also help us to achieve a different, more desirable form and culture of self-improvement?

My answer is positive: technologies are part of the problem, but they could also become part of the solution. We need different technologies, technologies that help us to achieve a different kind of self-knowledge and self-improvement: one that is not about quantity but quality, one that knows its own limits, and one that delivers a more sustainable and deeper kind of self-development, one that is as profound as the ones promoted by ancient wisdom traditions and humanism and as vital as those developed in non-Western cultures. We need technologies that help us to understand ourselves in a relational way and to see others as partners in personal but also communal and collective processes of self-improvement, which are linked to processes of improving our society. We need technologies that help us to generate new relations, new meanings, and new patterns of personal and collective growth. We need technologies that transform societies and create new, better cultures.

This way of putting it might sound strange because we are used to think of technology in ways that have nothing to do with self-development, society, and culture. But this is mistaken. Technology is entangled with human culture in various and complex ways. Technology is linked to ourselves, but also to the ways we do things together. Using terms from Wittgenstein, I have argued that technology is embedded in games and in a form of life.[1] When we use technologies, this is part of our activities and of the ways we do things in our society and culture. For example, when I use AI to do a search, this search is related to my activities (research, playing music, cooking, etc.) and the ways these activities are done in our society and culture: the rules, games, habits, norms, values, and so forth that are related to the activity. AI feeds on these, indirectly via data, and our interpretations of the results are embedded in those games and form of life. Similarly, humanist activities relied on a range of technologies and media—books, letters, the printing press—that were a crucial part in processes of making knowledge and interpreting, and that made sense only within a particular form of life.

Thus, technological use and activities do not take place outside of culture and society. Technologies are part of what we do and how we make sense, how we make meaning in a particular society and culture. Just as words have meaning only as they are used and within a particular language game and form of life, as Wittgenstein argued in his *Philosophical Investigations*, technologies such as books or AI make sense only within a larger social and cultural whole. And like the use of language, using technology is about communication, values, and meaning making. This is very clear when technology is directly connected to language use. For example, when my search involves autocorrect or when I use a translation app, it could be that problematic gender meanings slip in: the algorithm might default to male pronouns. But other technological activities such as driving a car or building a house are also embedded in a culture. For example, driving a car is embedded in a particular game that involves traffic rules and culturally accepted ways of doing. We seldom notice this when we are driving in our own country, but when we change country or learn to drive, we notice that we are also learning a slightly different or new culture: we have to learn to play a new game.

At the same time, technology also shapes and changes the game. It influences our values and our ways of doing things. Car technology has altered the way we live, for example by enabling commuting and hence creating particular geographical and sociological patterns. Or consider privacy: today, after years of using digital social media, we tend to be more willing to share private information. That kind of change is slow and hardly visible, but it is significant. There is no determinism; we can steer things to some extent and make changes to the game. And the relation between technologies and societies is complex.

Technologies and societies coevolve. Technology is not an external thing that shapes society; as we can learn from social studies of science and technology (STS), technology and society are deeply connected. But the role of technology in bringing about change is as crucial as the role of human decisions. Technologies give us different activities, different games, and in the end a different form of life. If we want to change the game, we therefore also have to change our technologies or at least use them in different ways. If we try to change our social institutions but do not deal with questions concerning technology, change will likely be superficial.

A good example of how important technologies are as co-shapers of society is the internet. The way we do things today, in our personal lives and at work, is so much shaped by internet and related digital technologies such as smartphones and apps that people who are born into this *culture* have difficulties imagining how it was possible to live one's life differently. The internet and the ecosystem of digital technologies that depend on it—including AI—turned and are still turning our society into a different one: a digital society, an internet society. The ways in which we live together and do things together is pervasively mediated by these digital technologies. Eventually, these technologies are no longer experienced as "new," since they have been integrated in, and transformed, our form of life. We no longer notice them because they are part of *how we do things here*. We have already stopped talking about "the internet"; it is part of our (life)world.

Self-improvement today *of course* involves the internet. That's not something we even notice: we search the internet on our computers or use apps. Older generations still had to adopt these technologies and this way of life. For millennials and Generation Z, it is the default, the world, the tradition, the starting point, and the horizon. Self-improvement takes place in that world and against that technocultural background. Young children are quickly initiated and absorbed into that culture. Learning the technology and learning the culture are no longer two entirely different things. There is no longer a gap between using digital technologies and making sense of and in this world. Only new technologies such as AI open this gap again. AI still opens what we could call *a hermeneutic gap*. First, it creates a meaning gap. We then try to make sense of the technology and we try to make sense when using the technology. We try to close that gap. We try to interpret what is going on. Since the technology is still new, we struggle to make sense of it and integrate it in our culture, which is already changing due to AI. We wonder how the hell we can know ourselves and improve ourselves in the light of the new possibilities offered by AI. There are books, exhibitions, and workshops about AI. This book can be interpreted as a contribution to that very cultural effort.

Another way of conceptualizing how technology is related to human culture and society is to say that technologies are linked to narratives. In the previous chapter, I already mentioned narratives when talking about the self. The self is a kind of story that we coauthor, interpret, and live. But narrativity is also important in relation to technology. This is most clear when we consider our stories about technology. We talk about technology in particular ways, which is shaped by narratives that are dominant in a particular social and cultural context. With regard to AI, currently these are competition narratives, including self-competition, and narratives about singularity and superintelligence. We are told that the United States and Europe have to compete with China in AI, for example. That AI is going to take over and create existential risks for humanity. That AI is going to solve all our problems, including poverty, war, and climate change. That we have to resist AI before it conquers us. That AI will turn us into numbers. That AI is going to help us to upgrade and enhance ourselves, improve ourselves by technological means. Often people ask me what AI is, or what I mean by AI. And the answer is not just a technical one. It is also one that involves stories. AI is technological and cultural at the same time.

112

Yet, since these stories also shape the development, use, and interpretation of AI, and since the stories in turn depend on the technological possibilities, these are not just stories *about* AI. Instead, there is a close entanglement between technologies and interpretation, technologies and meaning, technologies and culture. Our stories influence our technologies and vice versa. For example, the transhumanist story about superintelligence superseding humans was possible only because of accelerations in technological development: faster computing, more data. This technological progress made and makes people dream of a future in which AI reaches humanlike intelligence. That story in turns influences technological and scientific projects. And technology shapes the story of my life when through social media, for example, I come to understand my life as a series of events that can potentially be posted, that can get likes, and so on. Technology is not just a tool, an instrument. It also shapes my actions, my narratives, and thereby the meaning of life. Its narrative and hermeneutic power may be unintended and certainly underestimated; it may be invisible. But that does not mean it's not there.

If we want a different self-improvement culture, then, we need different stories and different technologies.

We need different stories about ourselves as societies and ourselves as persons. If we continue to believe in and indeed *live* the current narratives, there is little hope for social change. But if we start telling different stories, things are likely to change. For example, if we don't like the story that humans are a kind of machines and need to be upgraded, but at the same time continue to live our lives as if we are such machines and give credibility to people (in science, tech, and elsewhere) who promote this idea, then the narrative of our lives and our society is unlikely to change. Telling different stories about ourselves and reinterpreting and renarrating our history, present, and future, on the other hand, will contribute to such a change. If we don't like a particular story about AI and ourselves, then what we need to do is not just reject the story (let alone ignore it) but rewrite the story or write a new one. Faced with the current self-improvement culture, and indeed with the current culture as a whole, we need a new and better story about AI and about ourselves. Simply embracing an old one, say a Renaissance humanist story or Aristotelian story, won't do. We are condemned to make sense of ourselves here and now, to make sense of our own time. We may be inspired by old narratives, of course, and we always write against that horizon and have to respond to particular traditions, but if we want change—and we "have" to change and respond to change—we have no choice but to edit or write a new story. This is so at the personal level and at the level of a society and a culture. Self-improvement and self-change, understood as a hermeneutic project at personal and societal level, requires work: narrative work. I have to do that, we have to do that, it's my and our *hermeneutic responsibility*. That being said, we are never completely free and completely in control: we are "just" an important coauthor of our stories.

However, if I'm right that the relation between narratives and technology goes both ways, then it's not enough to change those narratives. We also need different technologies and media that give us different narratives, different societies, and different selves. Changing technology in order to change the self is possible and desirable because technologies are not just the passive objects of our narratives or the passive recorders of our stories: they also cocreate the narratives and cowrite the stories. For example, if the speed of modern life is indeed increasing, then that's not just because we tell each other that everything is going faster; it's also the computers, phones, calendars, emails, and so on that speed up our lives and that thus shape our stories and lifetimes. Technologies not only "function" and "work"; they also make meaning and change us and the way we do things, whatever they are intended for. They function and they operate, but they also narrate: they organize characters and events into a plot and enable us to find a new meaning. They are what Wessel Reijers and I have called "narrative technologies."[2] This can literally be the case. For example, my electronic calendar organizes my work life. Soon it might be organized by an AI algorithm, which will create a plot involving me, others, and events. AI will then shape my time and eventually my lifetime. But less literally, there is a sense in which technologies are not just objects in our world or tools in our hands but also shape the story of ourselves and our cultures. I already gave the example of social media. But technology also has this influence at a societal level. Just as industrial technologies created an industrial society or the internet created an internet society, AI is likely to create an AI society or data society—in fact, it is already doing so. Measured by the number of talks and stories we have about AI, it is becoming a core part of our culture, of our form of life, of the way(s) we do things.

More generally, technology is not just technical but also societal and cultural. If we tend to name our societies after technologies, there is a good reason for that: technologies are one of the central elements in the way we do things and in the way we life. Improving ourselves and improving society, then, are only possible if we change our technologies and media. To twist a famous formula from McLuhan: the medium is the narrative. Having new technologies means not only new messages but also new narratives. In this sense, AI tells us a different story. It creates a different story for us. If we want change, we can try to change the story, but we also need a different technology or a different kind of AI, a technology that cowrites a different story. If we don't like the way things go and if we really want to improve things and improve ourselves, we need a different coauthor.

Yet the author metaphor should not mislead us into thinking that AI is something entirely separate from us, that AI somehow stands "above" us as if it were a godlike author towering over us mortals. We should avoid talking about "technology" or "AI" as if it were something external to human culture. These technologies and media don't exert their influence in the form of humanlike artificial agents that dominate us, as if it were a kind of gods, overlords, or monsters; technologies such as AI shape our narratives by being interwoven with our lifeworld. Technologies are not aliens; they are human (but not humans) and are part of human culture. Or, to refer to an older narrative, technologies such as AI are not the enemy standing in front of the castle gate, as if they were an external threat; they are already long with us and within the walls. We can also use a biological-medical metaphor: technologies are like organisms, tissues, or drugs in the body. Inside the social body, technologies may help to sustain that society, but at the same time they can become a danger, depending on how they are programmed but also on the specific ways they interact with the rest of the social ecosystem and the environment. It is therefore not enough to simply say "change society" or even "change technology"; it is the entire sociotechnological ecology that needs to be changed. Like using the term "narrative technologies," talking about sociotechnological ecologies helps us to conceptually bind the social and technology together. We need more words that link technology to culture. "Narrative technologies" or "sociotechnological ecologies" are just some options.

Another option is to use the already existing term "technocultures," as I did throughout this book, because the technologies are connected to the ways we think and to the kind of social and cultural environment we live in. The term "technocultures" is especially helpful to emphasize the human role, the ways technologies are connected to humans and human culture. Technologies do not function just by themselves. We make them, use them, and interpret and narrate them. When it comes to self-development, it's always humans that have to be involved—and necessarily so. We are interpretative and relational beings who can and have to make sense of, and work on our relation to, ourselves, to others, and to the world. Human hermeneutic work is required. Decisions and control are also required. Yet this should not be an argument to say that "it all depends on what you do with the technology" and that it's about human goals alone. No technology or story is neutral. Independent of our intentions, they shape our goals and create new meanings. For example, nuclear technology gave us new military goals. Guns lead to shootings. The internet has created new subcultures and has transformed the mainstream culture. AI, in the form of self-driving cars, gives us new transportation goals. Future technologies can and will give us new technocultures. If we change AI or invent a new technology during the next decade, this will not only be a new tool; it will also change our aims, meanings, and culture.

Thus, if we want improvement of self and of society, then we need new stories, but we also need to shape a new technological and material basis for this change. This requires not just inward turns and self-reflection but also outward openness and—frankly speaking—work on things that have little to do with the self or even with "societies" or "cultures" in an abstract sense. In particular, it requires work on technologies: development of new technologies that can bring about social and cultural change or are at least embedded in a vision of such a change. Work on technologies, but while keeping in mind that this at the same time means work on our narratives, meanings, and values, work on our culture. Truly ambitious technology development should be understood not as a merely technological but a *technocultural* project. Inventors and entrepreneurs should ask themselves the question: Do I just want to make a new product, or do I want to change how we do things? Do I just want to offer a technological solution to a specific problem, or do I have the ambition to tell a new story? Like good art, good technology *can* change the way we see things and it can even change the world. It can *improve* things. It can also improve our stories and cowrite new stories. It can change the self. It can change personal and collective identity. And from a political point of view, as citizens we should ask if the technological "solutions" offered by the tech people and recommended by the advertisements lead to a story we want: a story we want to tell about ourselves as persons and as societies. If we don't like a particular story, we should take action to change it and take the role of coauthor. Writing the stories of ourselves and our societies should not be left to those who own, invest in, or develop AI and other technologies. Persons, communities, and societies should assume important roles as editors and coauthors. Technologies may be owned and developed by a small group of people. But what they do affects all of us. This gives us responsibilities and rights, as citizens, to co-shape those technological developments and make decisions about them. We may also want to rethink the way we organize ownership and development of technologies. After all, it's *our* technoculture, *our* society, and indeed *our* selves that are at stake.

TECHNOLOGY, STORIES, AND THE GOOD LIFE

However, this proposed shift from self-improvement, narrowly understood, to changing our society, changing our stories, and changing our technologies and technocultures, and indeed this more *political* interpretation of self-improvement does not imply that the ancient philosophical question regarding self-knowledge and the good life can or should be avoided. Rather, both should go together. Creating better narratives, better technologies, and better lives for ourselves and others needs some idea of what counts as "better." It needs what philosophers call "normative" direction. Here ethics comes in. Ancient ethics—from Western and non-Western traditions—can guide us when we search for what is good and better, for what counts as self-*improvement*.

But when it comes to technology, that's not just a one-way relation, a matter of application of existing ethics to technology. Technology can play an important role. It may help us with answering these ancient questions and in this way really support our relational autonomy and meaning making capacities instead of eroding them. Technologies and media could be our tools in that ancient philosophical quest, still so relevant today: to know ourselves and to discover and craft the good life. If it's right that technologies co-shape our culture, then let's experiment with new

119

technologies and *experience* and imagine how they (might) change our lives and societies. Today, and perhaps always, the question is not just "What is the good life?" but "What is the good life with technology?" With regard to AI, we thus have to ask: "What is the good life with AI?" Is the good life possible with AI, and if so how? What would be a good society with AI? What would be a *good* story? AI and data science, if we interpret them in a way that makes sense of its results, can help us to gain new self-knowledge. Even enhancement technologies can help us to explore new narrative-ethical possibilities. Exploring different selves and alternative ways of living need not imply that one has to return to an older way of living. Many so-called alternative communities adopt a neo-agrarian form of life. But this is just one possibility. We can also develop new technologies that enable new forms of life.

Yet the use of AI, positive psychology, or fast-track enhancement cannot *replace* the ancient question concerning self-knowledge and self-development. If the former are helpful at all, both need to go together. Thinking about new technologies, new stories, and better societies needs to be connected to thinking about human virtue and human flourishing. For example, as Shannon Vallor has proposed, we could ask what virtues technology ought to promote.[3] Following this line of inquiry, we could understand self-improvement as including ethical self-cultivation and ethical self-development and connect this with technology. Here AI presents dangers but may also offer opportunities. For example, Vallor is optimistic that quantified-self technology can also be used to achieve better self-awareness. I'm less sure about that: I have argued that AI gives us only a very specific kind of knowledge, which may be problematic. In addition, we also need human wisdom based on human experience and interpretation. But in any case, it is crucial to link the question of the good life to the question concerning technology.

However, ancient ethics and theory of self is not enough and raises its own problems, at least in its modern interpretation. Often Western virtue ethics is formulated in a way that makes it sounds as it is mainly about individual ethics and identity; it does not sufficiently emphasize what I have called in this book the *relational* self and the need for social and political change. Moreover, taking the relational approach further and taking into account environmental, posthumanist, and postmodern directions, neither flourishing nor self-improvement is merely a matter of improving humans. We should also think about what self-improvement and creating new stories and technologies means if we are no longer in the center, as selves and as humanity. We have to reflect on what it means for self and self-improvement that we are relational selves, that technology plays such an important role in our societies and in shaping the self, and that we have to live together with other, nonhuman beings on this earth. Ancient wisdom, humanist technologies, and Enlightenment ethics can help with the technocultural self-improvement project, but we have to do this exercise of self-narration and interpretation as the people we are here and now, and as people who are related to, and depend on, other beings, ecosystems, and technological systems. We also have to reinterpret what self-knowledge, wisdom, learning, autonomy, and improvement mean today, in this age with all its challenges (for example, systemic injustice and climate change) and in the light of current technologies such as AI. Therefore, we had better remain critical of the concepts of the past and become aware of their limitations. This includes being critical of ancient but also modern normative ideals. For example, we need to see the limitations of Stoicism and recognize that self-improvement is not a matter of absolute freedom and autonomy, as the radical Enlightenment and existentialism suggest, but can only be done in relation to others.

These "others" includes nonhumans. If we understand ourselves in a relational way, then purely anthropocentric notions of self-improvement should be criticized and overcome. There are not only human others on this planet but also nonhumans and natural environments. What I am, my story, needs to be connected to the story of other animals, ecosystems, the planet. In a radically relational view, my self-improvement depends on the improvement of those others and those environments. My improvement depends on *their* and that improvement. The "we" in "I am because we are, and since we are, therefore I am" needs to be extended. In this sense, any new digital humanism can only be a posthumanism and a postanthropocentrism. And this is also good for humans. Good lives need a good planet. Human flourishing requires the flourishing of nonhumans. We need to think about environmentally aware and "slow" forms of self-improvement and develop the required technologies for that. An environmental form of self-improvement. But with technology. Relationality also means recognizing the human relations to technology. Again, we need to acknowledge that technologies are not aliens or others but are made by humans and are coauthoring our human lives, narratives, and selves. We are not technologies, but we are technological. If authenticity has meaning at all, it is one that emerges from these cowritten narratives and relational projects of search for the good life and the good society. This seems a lot of work for one individual, too much work. But as I suggested in the previous chapter, luckily we are not alone in this quest for improvement. Self-improvement need not be a story of competing individuals. We can do this together. Together we can improve our narratives, our society, and our technologies, and thereby improve ourselves.

This approach challenges us to write better stories and build new and better technocultures for the twenty-first century. We cannot, and probably should not, go back to the past. We must reject a kind of Garden of Eden narrative, according to which technology led to a Fall and we now need to go back to a situation before technology. Such a situation does not exist and has never existed. We are technological by nature. But we improve things, and we can improve ourselves. We can change our narratives and our technologies to build a better world in which better selves and societies can grow. A world in which relations to other humans and to nonhumans are important. A world in which better selves and perhaps even more happy selves may be the welcome side-effect of better stories told by humans, their cultures, and their technologies.

With regard to AI, then, I propose that we change AI or develop new AI in such a way that it tells a different, better story of ourselves than our current ones. A better story than the neoliberal narrative about competition and markets. A better story than the transhumanist Dataism narrative promoted by current AI technology and its prophets. A story in which we can further develop and grow with the help of others and new technologies. A story in which we can make a different and better sense of the world we cocreate and in which we can take responsibility for what it becomes. A story in which we as persons and as humans are not necessarily the only protagonist and recognize that we do not and cannot fully know our own self, but also a story in which do not always get the feeling that we are not good enough in comparison to others or that we are totally insignificant in comparison to the new data gods that are supposed to be coming to overpower us. Humans often do stupid things, and there is much that can be improved and that needs to be improved. But often we do things that are good or good enough. We need a story for humans and mortals, not a story for machines or gods.

Furthermore, there are plenty of things that cannot be delegated to AI and computers or that we do not *want* to delegate to technology. And that's fine. Things have to make sense to us and for us. We are the sense-makers. When we write our stories for a better world, it is good to keep in mind that for some events and roles humans are required, and that humans are required for making sense of the stories, lives, and cultures as a whole. New meaning may emerge from the whole, of which technology is part and to which technology contributes, but that making and emerging of meaning happens always *through* human subjectivity. Technology is also an actor, what Latour called an *actant*. For example, AI can play the role of disruptor of the conversation or can take over tasks from humans. It may well coauthor stories. Elsewhere I have argued that technology choreographs, directs, and conducts us.[4] Technology shapes our (techno)culture in the ways I explained. Perhaps technology cocreates meaning. But we humans are the crucial editors of the stories and the mediators of meaning. AI, for all its merits and successes, cannot replace *that* role.

Perhaps we also need a story that dares again to use the "we" form, but then without making the mistakes of the past century. The particular ways in which technology and society have been combined in modern times in the name of a "we" are, and have been, disastrous. Technocultures of death and destruction have been legitimized by appealing to the rights of a people (*Volk*) or nation. But inhuman deeds and acts of mass destruction have also been done in and by states in the name of individual freedom. Both forms of individualism and collectivism are highly problematic, as are the modern culture and political ideologies that present us with this impossible choice. Yet without any kind of "we" there are no stories, no technologies, and ultimately also no self-improvement. In the previous chapter I argued that self-improvement requires social change and a political way of thinking. This seems to involve *some* kind(s) of "we." A focus on the individual self is not enough and does not make sense if viewed from a relational and societal point of view.

Now, it's not easy to figure out what this "we" could be. Academically and politically, there is much work to be done, and unfortunately thinking about politics and society is heavily underfunded and often relatively simplistic

125

compared to what goes on in other fields. This is disappointing and worrying in the light of the problems we face. But the solution is definitely not just: more technology. Social and political problems are very messy. They involve humans. They cannot be solved by means of numbers and statistics alone. The thought that AI can bypass all those difficult social and political challenges and that we can have technology without society is the beginning of the end. If AI, as technology and narrative, takes the form of technosolutionism, it leads to depoliticization of issues that should be treated in a political way and to a destruction of the public life. AI can contribute to dealing with societal problems but it is not the solution to everything. Technology can only be part of the solution; a broader political, societal, and (techno)cultural approach is needed. Similarly, a narcissistic turn to the self is disastrous, and the transhumanist desire to enhance and capture the self by means of technology is as misguided as the modern desire to leave no stone unturned in changing society. The current self-improvement crisis can be solved only if we stop worrying so much about improving our individual selves (or "the species," "the nation," and the like) and instead rethink and reshape both technologies and societies in light of a relational vision of the self, the good, the good society, and the good planet while building on the good things that are already happening and recognizing limitations to both knowledge and human action. This takes time and experience, but it's worth doing the work.

To conclude, we need to fundamentally rethink our guiding assumptions about self and self-improvement. We need a more relational and more political way of thinking about ourselves, which learns from ancient and non-Western thinking about the self, and which addresses the political-economic issues that lead to the current self-improvement crisis. We do not need more commercial self-help advice or "new" technologies that bring more of the same. Let's avoid the pitfalls of wellness capitalism and resist the promises of fast-track enhancement. Let's not just improve our position but change the game. Let's not be obsessed with changing ourselves; let's change society.

If we really want to improve ourselves, we need to care less about our "self" and instead focus on the good life and the good society, acquire wisdom based on experience instead of only collecting and analyzing data, understand ourselves in more relational ways that do justice to our dependencies on others, nonhumans, and technologies, contribute to making better societies and finding a new "we," develop better technologies and media than the ones we currently have, and create new stories that make sense of it all and contribute to a society and a technoculture worth wanting. Or, to put it in one sentence that emphasizes the active, narrative role of technology: we need technologies that tell different, better stories about us. Most likely, better "selves" will then emerge.

Notes

1. The Phenomenon: The Self-Improvement Imperative

1. Caroline Beaton, "Why Millennials Are Obsessed with Self-Improvement," *Psychology Today*, May 29, 2017, https://bit.ly/3E0bqVY.
2. Business Wire, "The U.S. Market for Self Improvement Products and Services," March 2, 2018, https://bwnews.pr/2Zz6a2C.
3. Derek Beres, "Self-Obsession Is Creating a Neurotic Culture. Can We Fix This?," *Big Think*, March 12, 2018, https://bigthink.com/culture-religion/self-obsession-is-creating-a-neurotic-culture-can-we-fix-this/.
4. Tina Edwards, "How Did We Become Obsessed with Self-Improvement?," Restlessnetwork.com, December 9, 2019, https://restlessnetwork.com/how-did-we-become-obsessed-with-self-improvement/.
5. Stephanie Brown, "Society's Self-Destructive Addiction to Faster Living," *New York Post*, January 4, 2014, https://bit.ly/3pUxDXO.
6. Will Storr, *Selfie: How We Became So Self-Obsessed and What It's Doing to Us* (New York: Abrams, 2018).
7. Thomas Henricks, "Self-Improvement as Cultural Illness," *Psychology Today*, January 10, 2016, https://bit.ly/3nEsHU2.
8. Alexandra Schwartz, "Improving Ourselves to Death," *New Yorker*, January 8, 2018, https://bit.ly/2Y2b2Nf.

9. Therese Hesketh, Q. J. Ding, and Rachel Jenkins, "Suicide Ideation in Chinese Adolescents," *Social Psychiatry and Psychiatric Epidemiology* 37 (2001): 230–235.
10. Arthur Miller, *Death of a Salesman* (New York: Penguin, 1976).
11. Liat Clark, "US Mass Shootings Blamed on High Gun Ownership and 'American Dream,'" *Wired*, August 24, 2015, https://bit.ly/3nIWlaI.
12. Dana Becker and Jeanne Marecek, "Dreaming the American Dream: Individualism and Positive Psychology," *Social and Personality Psychology Compass* 2, no. 5: 1767–1780, at 1770.
13. Gaston Franssen, "The Celebretization of Self-Care," *European Journal of Cultural Studies* 23, no. 1 (2020): 89–111.
14. Jonathan Crary, *24/7: Late Capitalism and the Ends of Sleep* (New York: Verso, 2014).
15. Shoshana Zuboff, *The Age of Surveillance Capitalism: The Fight for a Human Future at the New Frontier of Power* (New York: Public Affairs, 2019); Carl Cederström and André Spicer, *Desperately Seeking Self-Improvement: A Year Inside the Optimization Movement* (New York: OR Books, 2017).
16. Edwards, "How Did We Become Obsessed with Self-Improvement?"
17. See, for example, Stephanie Y. Evans, *Black Women's Yoga History: Memoirs of Inner Peace* (Albany: SUNY Press, 2021); Yasmin Tayag, "What I Gained from Self-Defense Class in the Wake of Anti-Asian Attacks," *New York Times*, June 9, 2021, https://nyti.ms/3jUxKi1; Megan Botel, "Native American Women Are Reclaiming Their Language," *Seattle Times* (April 19, 2021), https://bit.ly/3w3NfJf.

2. The History: Ancient Philosophers, Priests, and Humanists in Search of Self-Knowledge and Perfection

1. Epictetus, *Discourses and Selected Writings* (New York: Penguin, 2008).
2. Michel Foucault, *Technologies of the Self: A Seminar with Michel Foucault* (Amherst: University of Massachusetts Press), 19; Martha Nussbaum, *The Therapy of Desire: Theory and Practice in Hellenistic Ethics* (Princeton, NJ: Princeton University Press, 1994).
3. Michel Foucault, *The Use of Pleasure: The History of Sexuality, Volume 2* (New York: Penguin, 1992), 27.

4. Mitchell Dean and Daniel Zamora, *The Last Man Takes LSD: Foucault and the End of Revolution* (New York: Verso, 2021).

5. Foucault, *Technologies of the Self*, 18.

6. As many commentators point out, according to Buddhists, the self is an illusion and Enlightenment cannot be reached by forcing yourself. See, for example, this Reddit post: u/Timlikestturtles, "Self-Improvement vs. Buddhism," Reddit (accessed March 16, 2021), https://www.reddit.com/r/Buddhism/comments/se5r4/selfimprovement_vs_buddhism/; Mark Epstein, "Building a Better Self?," Lion's Roar (January 31, 2018), https://www.lionsroar.com/building-a-better-self/.

7. Peter Sloterdijk, *You Must Change Your Life* (Cambridge: Polity Press), 28.

8. Michel Foucault, *Confessions of the Flesh: The History of Sexuality, Volume 4* (New York: Pantheon Books).

9. Max Weber, *The Protestant Ethic and the Spirit of Capitalism* (London: Unwin Hyman, 1930).

10. Dean and Zamora use the term "entrepreneur of the self" when they talk about Foucault reading American neoliberals. See Weber, *The Protestant Ethic*. See also Mitchell Dean and Daniel Zamora, "The True Story of Michel Foucault's LSD Trip That Changed History," *Salon*, March 13, 2021, https://www.salon.com/2021/03/13/the-true-story-of-michel-foucaults-lsd-trip-that-changed-history/.

11. "Yes We Can" was a slogan used by the 2008 Barack Obama presidential campaign. Obama was seen as progressive but is nevertheless (still) neoliberal.

12. Peter Sloterdijk, "*Rules for the Human Zoo*: A Response to the Letter on *Humanism*," *Environment and Planning D: Society and Space D* 27, no. 1 (2009): 12–28, https://bit.ly/3nHFVPP.

13. Erika Rummel, "Desiderius Erasmus," *Stanford Encyclopedia of Philosophy*, updated October 14, 2021, https://stanford.io/3w00pdx.

14. Jean-Jacques Rousseau, *The Confessions* (London: Penguin, 1953).

15. Rousseau, *The Confessions*, 17.

16. Marshall McLuhan, *The Gutenberg Galaxy: The Making of Typographic Man* (Toronto: University of Toronto Press, 1962).

17. Rousseau, *The Confessions*.

18. Jean-Jacques Rousseau, *Emile, or On Education* (London: Penguin, 1979), 213–215.

19. Rousseau, *Emile*, 215.

20. Byung-Chul Han, *The Burnout Society* (Stanford, CA: Stanford University Press, 2015), 10.

3. The Society: Modern Self-Obsession from Rousseau to Hipster Existentialism

1. *Diagnostic and Statistical Manual of Mental Disorders*, 5th ed. (Washington, DC: American Psychiatric Association, 2013).

2. Sherry Turkle, *Alone Together: Why We Expect More from Technology and Less from Each Other* (New York: Basic Books, 2011). The quotations are at pages 56, 160, 177, and 179, respectively.

3. Jean M. Twenge and W. Keith Campbell, *The Narcissism Epidemic: Living in the Age of Entitlement* (New York: Atria Books, 2010), x.

4. Twenge and Campbell, *The Narcissism Epidemic*, 4.

5. Twenge and Campbell, *The Narcissism Epidemic*, 16–17.

6. Scott Barry Kaufman, "The Science of Spiritual Narcissism," *Scientific American*, January 11, 2021, https://www.scientificamerican.com /article/the-science-of-spiritual-narcissism/.

7. Christopher Lasch, *The Culture of Narcissism: American Life in an Age of Diminishing Expectations* (New York: Norton, 1979).

8. Christopher Lasch, "The Narcissist Society," *New York Review of Books* (September 30, 1976), https://www.nybooks.com/articles/1976/09 /30/the-narcissist-society/.

9. Allan Bloom, *The Closing of the American Mind* (New York: Simon & Schuster, 1987).

10. Fred Turner, *From Counterculture to Cyberculture* (Chicago: University of Chicago Press, 2006).

11. David Andrew, "Brand Revitalisation and Extension," in *Brands: The New Wealth Creators*, ed. Susannah Hart and John Murphy (Basingstoke, UK: Palgrave Macmillan), 189.

12. The Economist, "Mission Statement," June 2, 2009, https://econ.st /3GG6nly.

13. Mark Coeckelbergh, *New Romantic Cyborgs* (Cambridge, MA: MIT Press, 2017).

14. Eva Moskowitz, *In Therapy We Trust: America's Obsession with Self-Fulfillment* (Baltimore, MD: Johns Hopkins University Press, 2008).

15. Jean-Paul Sartre, *Existentialism Is a Humanism* (New Haven, CT: Yale University Press, 2007), 22.

16. Simone de Beauvoir, *The Second Sex* (New York: Vintage, 2011).

17. Beauvoir, *The Second Sex*, 36.

18. Olivia Goldhill, "Jean-Paul Sartre Was the Original Self-Help Guru," *Quartz*, May 13, 2018, https://qz.com/quartzy/1275452/most-self-help-ideas-were-written-first-and-better-by-jean-paul-sartre/.

19. Sartre, *Existentialism Is a Humanism*, 29.

20. Adam Grant, "Unless You're Oprah, 'Be Yourself' Is Terrible Advice," *New York Times*, June 4, 2016, https://nyti.ms/3nEKvym.

21. Charles Taylor, *The Ethics of Authenticity* (Cambridge, MA: Harvard University Press, 1991).

22. Somogy Varga and Charles Guignon, "Authenticity," in *Stanford Encyclopedia of Philosophy*, last updated September 20, 2020, https://stanford.io/3pShVfC.

23. The doctrine of non-self in Buddhism, indicated by the term *anatta* or *anatman*, says that there is no permanent self, soul, or essence.

24. Charles Taylor, *Sources of the Self: The Making of the Modern Identity* (Cambridge: Cambridge University Press, 1989), 462. See also Varga and Guignon, "Authenticity."

4. The Political Economy: Self-Taming and Exploitation Under Wellness Capitalism

1. Peter Sloterdijk, "*Rules for the Human Zoo*: A Response to the *Letter on Humanism*," *Environment and Planning D: Society and Space D* 27, no. 1 (2009): 12–28, https://journals.sagepub.com/doi/10.1068/dst3.

2. Friedrich Nietzsche, *Twilight of the Idols* (Indianapolis, IN: Hackett, 1997), 38.

3. Shoshana Zuboff, *The Age of Surveillance Capitalism* (New York: Public Affairs, 2019).

4. Herbert Marcuse, *One-Dimensional Man* (Boston: Beacon Press, 1964).

5. Global Wellness Institute, "Wellness Industry Statistics & Facts," https://globalwellnessinstitute.org/press-room/statistics-and-facts/.

6. Darko Jacimovic, "17 Powerful Self Improvement Industry Statistics," Deals on Health.net, September 3, 2020, https://dealsonhealth.net /self-improvement-industry-statistics/.

7. Caroline Beaton, "Why Millennials Are Obsessed with Self-Improvement," *Psychology Today*, May 29, 2017, https://www .psychologytoday.com/us/blog/the-gen-y-guide/201705/why -millennials-are-obsessed-self-improvement.

8. Rupert Neate, "Prince Harry Joins $1bn Silicon Valley Startup as Senior Executive," *The Guardian*, March 23, 2021, https://www .theguardian.com/uk-news/2021/mar/23/prince-harry-joins-1bn -silicon-valley-start-up-as-senior-executive.

9. Hester Bates, "Why Self-Development Creators Are Having a Moment in 2020," *The Drum*, October 9, 2020, https://www.thedrum.com /profile/influencer/news/why-self-development-creators-are-having -a-moment-in-2020.

10. Jessa Crispin, "Did I Use the Pandemic for 'Self-Improvement'? Nope. And That's Fine," *The Guardian*, June 16, 2021, https://www .theguardian.com/commentisfree/2021/jun/16/employers-think-the -pandemic-was-a-time-for-earnest-self-improvement-screw-that.

11. Bryce Gordon, "Self-Improvement and Self-Care: Survival Tactics of Late Capitalism," *Socialist Revolution*, March 12, 2018, https:// socialistrevolution.org/self-improvement-and-self-care-survival -tactics-of-late-capitalism/.

12. Gordon, "Self-Improvement and Self-Care."

13. Victor Tangermann, "Amazon Says Sad Workers Can Shut Themselves in 'Despair Closet': Inside the 'AmaZen' Box, Nobody Can Hear You Scream," *Futurism* (May 28, 2021), https://futurism.com/amazon -workers-despair-closet.

14. Gordon Hull and Frank Pasquale, "Toward a Critical Theory of Corporate Wellness," *Biosocieties* 13, no. 1 (2018): 190–212.

15. Christian Fuchs, *Digital Labour and Karl Marx* (New York: Routledge, 2014).

16. Nick Dyer-Witheford, Atle Mikkola, and James Steinhoff Kjøsen, *Inhuman Power: Artificial Intelligence and the Future of Capitalism* (London: Pluto Press, 2019), 11.

17. Stephen Johnson, "This New Hyperloop Pod Could Get You from L.A. to San Francisco in 30 Minutes," World Economic Forum, October 11, 2018, https://www.weforum.org/agenda/2018/10/new-700-mph-hyperloop-pod-can-go-from-l-a-to-san-francisco-in-30-minutes/.

18. Jason Tebbe, "Twenty-First Century Victorians," *Jacobin*, October 31, 2016.

5. The Technology: Categorized, Measured, Quantified, and Enhanced, or Why AI Knows Us Better Than Ourselves

1. Mark Coeckelbergh, *New Romantic Cyborgs* (Cambridge, MA: MIT Press, 2017).

2. See Deborah Lupton, *The Quantified Self* (Cambridge: Polity Press, 2016).

3. Flavio Luis de Mello and Sebastiao Alves de Souza, "Psychotherapy and Artificial Intelligence: A Proposal for Alignment," *Frontiers in Psychology* 10 (2019): 263, https://www.frontiersin.org/articles/10.3389/fpsyg.2019.00263/full.

4. Sherry Turkle, "Artificial Intelligence and Psychoanalysis: A New Alliance," *Daedalus* 117, no. 1 (1988): 241–268.

5. Katie Aafjes-van Doorn et al., "A Scoping Review of Machine Learning in Psychotherapy Research," *Psychotherapy Research* 31, no. 1 (2021): 92–116, https://www.tandfonline.com/doi/full/10.1080/10503307.2020.1808729.

6. Yuval Noah Harari, *Homo Deus* (London: Vintage, 2015), 392.

7. Harari, *Homo Deus*, 393.

8. Pico della Mirandola, "Oration on the Dignity of the Human Being," Panarchy.org, https://www.panarchy.org/pico/oration.html.

9. John Harris, *Enhancing Evolution: The Ethical Case for Making Better People* (Princeton, NJ: Princeton University Press, 2007).

10. See, for example, Barbara J. Sahakian and Julia Gottwald, *Sex, Lies & Brain Scans: How fMRI Reveals What Really Goes On In Our Minds* (Oxford: Oxford University Press, 2017).

11. Ray Kurzweil, "The Coming Merging of Mind and Machine," *Scientific American* February 1, 2008, https://bit.ly/3BwjnGL.

12. Julian Savulescu and Hannah Maslen, "Moral Enhancement and Artificial Intelligence: Moral AI?," in *Beyond Artificial Intelligence*, ed. Jan Romportl, Eva Zackova, and Jozef Kelemen (Cham, Switzerland: Springer International, 2015), 79–95.

13. Francisco Lara and Jan Deckers, "Artificial Intelligence as a Socratic Assistant for Moral Enhancement," *Neuroethics* 13 (2020): 275–287.

14. The use of binaural soundscapes is said to shift consciousness.

15. Thobey Campion, "How to Escape the Confines of Time and Space According to the CIA," *Vice*, February 16, 2021, https://www.vice.com /en/article/7k9qag/how-to-escape-the-confines-of-time-and-space -according-to-the-cia.

16. Giuseppe Riva et al., "Transforming Experience: The Potential of Augmented Reality and Virtual Reality for Enhancing Personal and Clinical Change," *Frontiers in Psychiatry* 7 (2016): 164, https://www.ncbi .nlm.nih.gov/pmc/articles/PMC5043228/.

6. The Solution (Part I): Relational Self and Social Change

1. The concept of the uncanny was introduced by Ernst Jentsch and developed by Sigmund Freud in his 1919 essay "Das Unheimliche."

2. Jacques Lacan, *Écrits*, trans. Bruce Fink (New York: Norton, 2006), 224. For a reflection on extimate technologies, see Hub Zwart, "Extimate Technologies and Techno-Cultural Discontent," *Techné: Research in Philosophy and Technology* 21, no. 1 (2017): 24–54, and Ciano Aydin, *Extimate Technology* (New York: Routledge, 2021).

3. John Trudy, *The Anatomy of Story* (New York: Farrar, Straus and Giroux, 2007).

4. Paul Ricoeur, *Time and Narrative, Volume 1*, trans. Kathleen McLaughlin and David Pellauer (Chicago: University of Chicago Press, 1984).

5. Charles Taylor, *Sources of the Self* (Cambridge: Cambridge University Press, 1989), 47.

6. Charles Taylor, *The Ethics of Authenticity* (Cambridge, MA: Harvard University Press, 1991), 39.

7. Alasdair MacIntyre, "The Claims of After Virtue," *Analyse & Kritik: Zeitschrift für Sozialwissenschaften* 6, no. 1 (May 1, 1984): 3–7, reprinted

in *The MacIntyre Reader*, ed. Kelvin Knight (Notre Dame, IN: University of Notre Dame Press),71–72.

8. For example, Carol Gilligan's seminal work on women's development offers a relational view of moral development that emphasizes care of others rather than principled ways of reasoning as the highest stage of moral development. Carol Gilligan, *In a Different Voice: Psychological Theory and Women's Development* (Cambridge, MA: Harvard University Press, 1982). See also Judith V. Jordan, "The Relational Self: A New Perspective for Understanding Women's Development," in *The Self: Interdisciplinary Approaches*, ed. Jaine Strauss and Georg R. Goethals (New York: Springer, 1991), 137–149.

9. See, for example, Chenyang Li, "The Confucian Ideal of Harmony," *Philosophy East and West* 56, no. 4 (2006): 583–603.

10. John S. Mbiti, *African Religions and Philosophy* (Nairobi: East African Educational Publishers, 1969), 108–109.

11. Gilles Deleuze, "Post-Script on Societies of Control," *October* 59 (1992): 3–7.

12. Deleuze, "Post-Script on Societies of Control," 6.

13. Bruno Latour, *We Have Never Been Modern* (Cambridge, MA: Harvard University Press, 1993).

14. For more on technology and vulnerability, see Mark Coeckelbergh, *Human Being @ Risk* (New York: Springer, 2013).

15. Karen Karbo, *Yeah, No. Not Happening: How I Found Happiness Swearing Off Self-Improvement and Saying F*ck It All—and How You Can Too* (New York: Harper Wave, 2020).

16. For a discussion of the political-philosophical challenges in terms of liberty, see Mark Coeckelbergh, *Green Leviathan, or the Poetics of Political Liberty* (New York: Routledge, 2021).

17. For more on intentional communities, see, for example, Mike Mariani, "The New Generation of Self-Created Utopias," *New York Times*, January 16, 2020, https://nyti.ms/3BLC2yB.

18. Martin Heidegger, *The Question Concerning Technology, and Other Essays* (New York: Harper & Row, 1977).

19. For an overview, see Mark Coeckelbergh, *Introduction to Philosophy of Technology* (New York: Oxford University Press, 2019).

7. The Solution (Part II): Technologies That Tell Different Stories About Us

1. Mark Coeckelbergh, *Using Words and Things* (Abingdon, UK: Routledge, 2017).

2. The term "narrative technologies" was first used as a technical term in work I did with Wessel Reijers, but in this book I use the term more broadly. See, for example, Mark Coeckelbergh and Wessel Reijers, "Narrative Technologies," *Human Studies* 39 (2016): 325–346, https://link.springer.com/article/10.1007%2Fs10746-016-9383-7.

3. Shannon Vallor, *Technology and the Virtues: A Philosophical Guide to a Future Worth Wanting* (New York: Oxford University Press, 2018).

4. Mark Coeckelbergh, *Moved by Machines* (New York: Routledge, 2019).

Index

INDEX

INDEX